THE LIBRARY OF HOLOCAUST TESTIMONIES

I was No. 20832 at Auschwitz

The Library of Holocaust Testimonies

Editors: Antony Polonsky, Martin Gilbert CBE, Aubrey Newman,
Raphael F. Scharf, Ben Helfgott

Under the auspices of the Yad Vashem Committee of the Board of
Deputies of British Jews and the Centre for Holocaust Studies,
University of Leicester

My Lost World by Sara Rosen
From Dachau to Dunkirk by Fred Pelican
Breathe Deeply, My Son by Henry Wermuth
My Private War by Jacob Gerstenfeld-Maltiel
A Cat Called Adolf by Trude Levi
An End to Childhood by Miriam Akavia
A Child Alone by Martha Blend
I Light a Candle by Gena Turgel
My Heart in a Suitcase by Anne L. Fox
Memoirs from Occupied Warsaw, 1942–1945
by Helena Szereszewska
Have You Seen My Little Sister?
by Janina Fischler-Martinho
Surviving the Nazis, Exile and Siberia by Edith Sekules
Out of the Ghetto by Jack Klajman with Ed Klajman
From Thessaloniki to Auschwitz and Back 1926–1996
by Erika Myriam Kounio Amariglio
Translated by Theresa Sundt
I Was No.20832 at Auschwitz by Eva Tichauer
Translated Colette Lévy and Nicki Rensten
My Child is Back! by Ursula Pawel
Wartime Experiences in Lithuania by Rivka Lozansky Bogomolnaya
Translated by Miriam Beckerman

I Was
No. 20832
at Auschwitz

EVA TICHAUER

translated by
Colette Lévy and Nicki Rensten
Preface by Ethel Tolansky, Group for War and
Culture Studies, University of Westminster

VALLENTINE MITCHELL
LONDON • PORTLAND, OR

First published in French in 1988 by
EDITIONS L'HARMATTAN
16 rue des Ecoles
Paris 75005

Published in 2000 in Great Britain by
VALLENTINE MITCHELL
Newbury House, 900 Eastern Avenue
London, IG2 7HH

and in the United States of America by
VALLENTINE MITCHELL
c/o ISBS, 5804 N.E. Hassalo Street
Portland, Oregon 97213-3644

Website: www.vmbooks.com

British Library Cataloguing in Publication Data
    Tichauer, Eva
        I was number 20832 at Auschwitz. – (The library of
        Holocaust testimonies)
        1. Tichauer, Eva 2. Auschwitz (Concentration camp)
        3. Holocaust, Jewish (1939–1945) – Personal narratives
        I. Title
        94.5¢318¢092

        ISBN 0-85303-396-X
        ISSN 1363-3759

Library of Congress Cataloging-in-Publication Data

    Tichauer, Eva.
        [J'étais le numéro 20832 à Auschwitz. English]
        I was number 20832 at Auschwitz/Eva Tichauer;
        translated by Colette Lévy and Nicki Rensten.
            p. cm.
        ISBN 0-85303-396-X (pbk)
        1. Tichauer, Eva. 2. Jews–Persecutions–France–Paris–Biography.
        3. Holocaust, Jewish (1939–1945)–France–Paris–Personal narratives.
        4. Paris (France)–Biography.
        I. Title

        DS135.F9 T5313 2000
        940.53¢18¢094436–dc21   00-056619

Printed by Creative Print and Design, (Wales), Ebbw Vale.

For Jeanette and Didier, my children

The Last Poem

I dreamt so much of you
I walked so much, spoke so much
Loved your shadow so much
That nothing remains of you.
It only remains for me to be a shadow
among shadows
To be a hundred times more shadow than the shadow
To be the shadow that will come again and again
in your life full of sunshine.

Robert Desnos, 1945

The Library of Holocaust Testimonies

It is greatly to the credit of Frank Cass that this series of survivors' testimonies is being published in Britain. The need for such a series has long been apparent here, where many survivors made their homes.

Since the end of the war in 1945 the terrible events of the Nazi destruction of European Jewry have cast a pall over our time. Six million Jews were murdered within a short period; the few survivors have had to carry in their memories whatever remains of the knowledge of Jewish life in more than a dozen countries, in several thousand towns, in tens of thousands of villages, and in innumerable families. The precious gift of recollection has been the sole memorial for millions of people whose lives were suddenly and brutally cut off.

For many years, individual survivors have published their testimonies. But many more have been reluctant to do so, often because they could not believe that they would find a publisher for their efforts.

In my own work over the past two decades, I have been approached by many survivors who had set down their memories in writing, but who did not know how to have them published. I realized what a considerable emotional strain the writing down of such hellish memories had been. I also realized, as I read many dozens of such accounts, how important each account was, in its own way, in recounting aspects of the story that had not been told before, and adding to our understanding of the wide range of human suffering, struggle and aspiration.

With so many people and so many places involved, including many hundreds of camps, it was inevitable that the historians and students of the Holocaust should find it difficult at times to grasp the scale and range of the events. The publication of memoirs is therefore an indispensable part of the extension of knowledge, and of public awareness of the crimes that had been committed against a whole people.

Martin Gilbert
Merton College, Oxford

Contents

Biographical Note   viii

Foreword   ix

Preface by Ethel Tolansky   xi

1   The Great Round-up of 16 July 1942   1
2   Berlin–Paris   4
3   Drancy   15
4   Birkenau   21
5   *Stabsgebäude* Auschwitz   53
6   *Taraxacum Kok-Saghiz*   58
7   Death March   78
8   Ravensbrück   80
9   Malchow   82
10   Leipzig   84
11   The Final March   86
12   The Taste of Freedom   90
13   The Return   93
Epilogue   96

Biographical Note

Eva Tichauer was born in Berlin at the end of the First World War. She and her family emigrated to Paris in 1933. After the Second World War Eva completed her medical studies and qualified as a doctor. No longer practising, she is now very involved in work for the Fédération Nationale des Déportés, Internés, Résistants et Patriotes (FNDIRP), fighting for peace, disarmament and the development of the Third World.

Foreword

Auschwitz was the turning point in my life, the end of my youth and my illusions. I hadn't done anything special to deserve such a history lesson. I regret to say that I was one of the *innocente*.

This experience of inhumanity and humanity, of atrocities and superhuman survival, of hatred and love, drove me to swear to myself that if I survived, I would dedicate my rebirth to proving myself worthy of my deportation.

If now I decide, more than 40 years after my liberation, to re-open my wounds and add my own testimony to those of my comrades who have already shown that courage, it is because I have a duty to do so.

I owe it to my parents, Theodor and Erna, who perished in the Holocaust and without whom I would not have become the person I am. They can survive only through me.

I owe it to my comrades who died in the lucrative death factories, the industrial extermination, the multiple genocide, which was our shared hell. We promised them we would reveal everything if we ever returned.I owe it to my adopted children for whom I was only able to provide a rootless mother and no other family.

I owe it to the young, who are the age I was then, and who ask me in debates: 'How did you survive in an extermination camp?' or 'Tell us what happened to you personally' or 'Can one overcome such a terrible past?'These questions deserve an answer. I think you can only address others when you speak from the heart, when you can look into the eyes of the person you are answering.

I owe it, finally, to the solemn declaration made in the camps, when we stood in the yards for our roll calls and the doors re-opened to a reconquered liberty, of which we wanted to be the future guardians: 'Never again! Let's remain

From that time on, to remain in harmony with the lessons of Auschwitz, I committed myself for ever and with all my will to that single vision of a future called faithfulness and solidarity, peace and brotherhood.

I am just one link in an endless humanity. As both my present, which I live to the full, and my future, of which I know neither the depth nor the duration, are dependent on this past, I will speak of my individual journey to the death camps. From Berlin to Paris, from Paris to the depths of barbarism, in the midst of the civilised world. To survive, one piece of good luck was not enough; you needed many. Throughout this travelogue the instances of good fortune I experienced are the thread which runs through my story.

I am not writing for myself or for those who went through the same experienced, but to enlighten the generations which come after me and which are in search of their own future. Knowledge of the past is indispensable to the construction of the future.

Preface

Eva Tichauer wrote about her wartime experiences almost forty-three years after her return to France from her ordeal at Auschwitz and elsewhere, when she was 70 years old. The time gap has not blurred her memories nor her sense of purpose in writing down what happened to her and others from the moment of her arrest and throughout her time spent in deportation. Her overriding preoccupation has been and still is to make people, especially the young, aware of the courage and endurance displayed by the prisoners in the face of suffering on the one hand, and the capacity for inflicting suffering displayed by the SS guards and their masters on the other. Eva has committed herself to ensuring that the horrific events of the concentration camps are not repeated. After reading her book one feels impelled to make a similar commitment to ensure that human beings never again have to suffer the same ignominies, the physical abuse and the denial of the right to live, on such a horrific scale. However, we know that in our contemporary political life there is a continuing reappearance, growth and development of negationism in relation to the Holocaust, the concentration camps and Nazism itself. This negationism exists not only in the contentions of `historians' but, as recent political events have shown in Europe, it also forms part of a revival of extreme racist ideas that seem to have followers in spite of all that has been written and shown about the horrors of the Second World War. It is therefore ever more necessary for those survivors who feel that they can write down the painful memories of the past to do so; and for the reading public to be more aware than ever that the evil of the camps and the ideologies behind them are still smouldering below the surface in our society.

There can never be enough Holocaust and concentration camp testimonies, as the voice behind each one is personal and the circumstances different. Eva captures the solidarity of the women enduring indescribable physical sufferings and affronts to their dignity; their fortitude; and their desperate will to survive in circumstances that after so many years have passed, seem beyond belief. Survival itself was a matter of chance. In her case, a certain amount of medical knowledge made number 20832 useful, and therefore not so easily disposable as someone else. This fact, as well as that of having witnessed the deaths of so many others in the various camps she was sent to, places a heavy burden of memory on the survivor and also, as Eva saw it, a responsibility towards those who did not survive.

The book is about survival, not only in the camps but afterwards in the land of the living. How does one remake one's life after returning from the descent into the abyss? How does one come to terms with rebuilding the self when there has been a very careful, well-thought-out and organized plan to reduce the human being to the level of an animal or a corpse and when, especially in the case of women, scientific experiments were carried out which denied them the possibility of having children?

Eva, the sole survivor out of her family, fought to make herself a `new' life, one that was full of optimism and understanding, a proactive life in very many respects. She completed her medical studies, became a doctor, adopted two children, and now gives herself unstintingly to sharing her experiences with younger generations in order to preserve a sense of the respect for life and human dignity in the face of individual and collective amnesia, voluntary or otherwise, in today's society.

I Was No. 20832 at Auschwitz is not a day-to-day diary but rather a chronological development of Eva's experiences, linked to those of others who were with her in the many different camps with their peculiar and particular regimes from 1942 to her liberation. She tells of her life during that time with a controlled realism that makes the effects even stronger. A caring for others and a fighting spirit fill the pages, as well as moments of disbelief that such atrocities were possible and an overall lack of revenge or vindictiveness. However, for all her optimism and love of life, Eva would be the first to admit that the after-effects remain with her. My awareness of all this made meeting Eva a few years ago a deeply-felt experience. She is a really remarkable person, full of zest for life and fighting spirit, always thinking of new projects in a positive and out-going way. Colette Lévy and Nicki Rensten have done wonderful work on the translation. It is encouraging to know that through their efforts this book will now reach a wider audience and help to fulfil Eva's own words: 'Knowledge of the past is indispensable to the construction of the future'.

Ethel Tolansky
Group For War and Culture Studies,
University of Westminster.

1 · The Great Round-up of 16 July 1942

In the beginning there was 16 July 1942. At 7 a.m. the bell rings at our door in the district of Les Batignolles. I am lying next to my mother in the twin bed where my father used to sleep before his arrest on 12 December 1941.

We have been awake for a long time, and have taken stock for the last time. We were expecting this call. We knew that never again would the bakery boy from the rue des Moines come to that door to deliver our buns and croissants as he did before the war.

Some friends had warned us by telephone the day before that terrible things were in the making, that we needed to run away, if there was still time, to go into hiding ourselves, at least not to open the door to anyone. It was more than a piece of advice; it was a whispered command.

Our shutters are closed; it's too late to hide. Not opening the door is still possible. Our suitcases are ready for I do not know what journey. A few gold coins are sewn into the hems of our dresses. We are poor immigrant women but my mother is far-sighted.

My mother loves my father and dreams of joining him. He left Compiègne on 27 March in the first transportation of prominent Jews arrested a few months earlier.[1] I never saw him again. My mother wanted to be alone at each attempted encounter, successful or not. I retain the image of a living father!

On the previous 5 May, according to a solid family tradition, I offered my mother some flowers for their wedding anniversary. It was their silver wedding. My mother never

1

learnt that my father was already dead. I was to learn it officially five years later with a precise date: 6 April 1942, about ten days after his arrival.

In the hope of eventually receiving news of my father, we never left the rue Nollet. Such news could only arrive at our home, a home we had re-created only a few years earlier, when we fled Hitler's Germany in 1933.

I wait for my mother's decision: 'Go and open the door.' I obey. On the doorstep are two French policemen, one in plain clothes, the other in uniform.

We are soon ready. My mother has prepared a leather briefcase with documents and family photographs. She asks whether I can take it downstairs to the concierge's. Permission is given. There is only one flight of stairs to go down. Does mother want me to run away? The Metro Brochant is very near. Today I am convinced of it, but at the time I did not understand. My mother then had only me; I could not abandon her. I went upstairs again, perhaps to the surprise of the policemen, and we followed them together, in the first instance to the town hall of the 17th Arrondissement.

Early in the morning we find ourselves at the Salle Wagram where, in the hours which will follow, we will see the foreign Jews of the district pour in.

Curious coincidence. For me this is no ordinary hall. This place is a synagogue. The Association of German Jewish Immigrants in France whose president was my father, rented this hall for years, to celebrate among ourselves the Jewish New Year and *Yom Kippur* (Day of Atonement).

Closing my eyes, I remember my surprise at the sight of my father dressed like a believer, carrying the Torah and able to chant in Hebrew, which had vanished from my childhood memories since the *Kiddush*[2] of my grandfather. This incomprehensible language became familiar. I was choked with emotion.

I can also smell the apple stuck with cloves that my mother

had prepared for me so I would tolerate my first *Yom Kippur* fast more easily. My mother even knew how to write Hebrew. I held her tight in my arms and sang in my head, 'Hear, oh Israel, the Lord thy God, the Lord is One'. We were not believers, but religion is a bond in the sorrow of immigration.

At the end of the day a bus took us straight to Drancy. We didn't pass through the winter sports stadium, the famous Vel d'Hiv. This was my first piece of luck. I am today, perhaps, the only surviving woman from the great round-up of the Vel d'Hiv of 16–17 July 1942, even though I never actually went there.

NOTES

1. See Serge Klarsfeld *Le Mémorial de la déportation des juifs de France: Convoi no.1*, (Memorial to the Deportation of the Jews of France: Convoy Number 1).
2. Celebration on Friday evenings of the start of the Sabbath, day of rest for the Jews.

2 • *Berlin–Paris*

We had been German for several generations, long enough to be perfectly assimilated. We spoke Hochdeutsch and not Yiddish. Abandoning the religion of their ancestors, my father and mother called themselves free-thinkers and claimed for themselves Goethe, Kant and Spinoza.

After a seven-year engagement, due to a protracted war, my father, who had not killed anyone and was proud of it, obtained special leave in May 1917 to get married. I was born nine months later.

After the armistice and the birth of the Weimar Republic, by mutual agreement and in a quest for greater social justice, my parents joined the SPD (German Social Democratic Party). From the time I became aware of their political involvement, I always saw them active in the 57th Berlin branch, and my father also in the *Reichsbanner* ex-servicemen's association (1924–33), against chauvinistic and revanchist militarism. Until their premature end, they remained faithful to the hope of socialism. As early as possible, I followed them on this road into the Red Falcons and the Socialist Youth.

I remember that after the death of Friedrich Ebert, the first and only social-democratic president of the Weimar Republic, they voted for Otto Braun against Marshal von Hindenburg, but also against the union with the KPD (German Communist Party) of Ernst Thaelmann and the *Rote Front* that he advocated.

I did not understand at the time that the visceral anti-communism of German social democracy was going to allow the nationalist right to choose the man capable of turning the masses into fanatics; of enrolling the millions of the Republic's unemployed alongside their class enemies thanks to the soup

4

kitchens and the brown shirts; seducing the youth with his demagogic and incendiary speeches; and convincing the bankers and the big industrialists of the Ruhr and Silesia that they would draw the largest profits through their financial support. Adolf Hitler was their man and their pressure forced the old marshal to summon him legally to the *Reich*'s chancellorship.

In his book *Mein Kampf*, Hitler had designated 'the Jews' as the scapegoats, responsible for all the ills of Germany. His anti-Semitic, racist theories were to strengthen the belief that the 'Aryans' were a race of lords, chosen to become the masters of the world.

Professionally, my father would not finish his law studies until 1920, the year of the birth of my brother Félix, who was named after an uncle killed on the Somme.

The house at 137 Kantstrasse, where I spent a happy child-hood, was destroyed during the war. We shared a flat there with my father's parents, and the flat also housed my father's barrister's chambers, and later on the solicitor's practice as well, a right which was granted to war veterans after a period of five years.

Deprived of higher education by the premature death of her father, my mother had become an excellent shorthand secretary. After having worked at the AEC (*Allgemeine Electrizitätsgesellschaft*) during the war, she was perfectly capable of running her husband's chambers, taking an interest in the law and acquiring, when I went to the lycée, a certificate and a degree in law.

As a barrister, my father acted for the *Deutsche Gewerkschaftsbund* (German Trades Union Congress) and as a solicitor signed the deeds with which citizens had to show that they expressly wanted to leave the religious community indicated on their birth certificates in order not to be taxed for it, as there was no separation of church and state in Weimar

Germany. These two professional activities were enough for my father to be struck off the Berlin Bar when Hitler came to power.

Meanwhile, I went happily to school. My grandmothers told me fairy tales; my grandfather, a teacher of Judaism in a grammar school, read the Bible to me. And, as ultimately my ancestors were neither Germans nor Gauls, I accepted the family oral tradition by which I was a descendant of Levi, son of Jacob and Lea, by my Ashkenazi father, and of King David by my Sephardi mother. The former had come from Poland and Russia, fleeing the pogroms, the latter from Spain at the time of the heretic-burners of the Inquisition.

With my blue eyes and my blond plaits, I looked like a German '*Gretschen*', but for Hitler, his SA and SS, we were judeo-bolsheviks of an inferior race.

After the *Reichstag* fire, which they accused the communists of starting in order to ban their party, when historically the real pyromaniac was Hermann Goering, events developed very fast.

From 1 April, they daubed black circles on the professional plaques at the entrance of the house. We almost left the same day for London. But my father could easily prove that he was not really a communist. He hoped to get the right to practise on account of his second-class iron cross – no first class for the Jews in Prussia who could not become officers. My mother was decorated too: she had given some gold to forge German steel for the war in 1914–18. This hope delayed our departure by three months, the exact time which separated the banning of the KPD from the banning of the SPD.

This lapse of time changed our destination and the destiny of the family. Putting our trust in the revolutionary history of the French people, we arrived at the Gare de l'Est in the evening of 27 July 1933. At midnight we found ourselves on the hill of Montmartre, contemplating the City of Light at our feet. We were overwhelmed. France had become our land of asylum, our second homeland, freely chosen.

To integrate into French society, my father tried first to believe that every Jew had a knack for trade. It is untrue. He failed very soon with his small enterprise in Clichy. It was based in a garage, where he made attempts at producing Bakelite saucers showing the price of the beverage to sell to bistros in Paris. He didn't manage to sell them: there was too much competition.

Then he was forced to go back to the level of the baccalauréat and recommence law studies at the Sorbonne whilst studying French at the Alliance Française.

There was an economic and political rule aimed at reducing the number of immigrant intellectuals by transforming them into skilled workers at evening classes. When he was called up, my father was sent to a class to train as a fitter. He was proud of the spare parts he brought home and I was full of admiration for the metal pieces which interlocked with precision. But the teachers must have passed a more severe judgement on the capability of my father to become a worker.

He remained an intellectual with a knowledge of the law. And so he became one of the most trusted legal advisors in France working for German, mostly Jewish, immigrants. Fees for this work were uncertain and impossible to count on.

My mother, with a more adaptable profession, became first secretary to Georg Bernard, chief editor of the German immigrant daily paper. Later on, she found a more regular job at the World Jewish Congress with Nahum Goldmann.

Our family budget relied on my mother's regular salary and the variable earnings of my father. We managed to live frugally and my mother used to say: 'One must live according to one's situation, dress above one's situation and eat below one's situation.'

I was judged only good enough to undertake a long period of study. When I resumed school in 1933–34 I made more than five mistakes in dictation in the entrance examination for the fourth-year classics stream of the Lycée Jules Ferry, Place Clichy. The resultant zero mark made me go back to the third-year class. At the end of the year, having gained a prize for excellence, I passed my examination quite easily and, with the agreement of my teachers, moved up to the fifth year before the summer holidays.

Following this I had to leave my family for two years, returning home only during the holidays. This was firstly for financial reasons. But also, in order to learn French better and get rid of my accent, I needed a complete immersion in the language. In my family, we carried on speaking German among ourselves.

I was sent as an *au pair* to the home of a couple of Jewish doctors of Russian origin, where I had to supervise the studies of an adopted son, a bit of a dunce, who was a fourth-year pupil and at the same time I pursued my own studies.

At the lycée Jeanne d'Arc, in Orléans, an understanding headmistress allowed me to sit for the examination to move up to the sixth year. A number of teachers in Paris and Orléans helped me to jump from the third to the sixth year. I got a 'B' pass in the first part of the baccalauréat.

The following year, thanks to the generosity of French, Jewish and freemason friends, I became a boarder at the lycée Jeanne d'Arc, happy to be rid of my idiotic pupil. But at the lycée for girls, there was no question of opening a class in elementary mathematics for only three young candidates. Two families solved the problem for their daughters with private lessons. I was the only girl to enter the lycée F. Pothier for boys. I still remember with emotion my first May Day lily-of-the-valley offered to me collectively by my male schoolmates. It was the year of the victory of the Popular Front.

I failed my maths due to viral hepatitis; I was stuck in the infirmary for the duration of the paper on the mechanics of vectors. But I passed philosophy, which I sat at the same time and which I had prepared on my own, although I did not get a distinction due to my optional authors. Alongside Descartes and Kant, I had chosen Spinoza, the Jew, whose *Ethics* and *Quod Erat Demonstrandum* did not particularly appeal to my examiner. He then wanted to question me on metaphysics, which did not appeal to me.

The main thing was that the gates of the university were now open to me.

I was able, finally, to return home to my parents and enrol for the Physics, Chemistry and Biology course at Jussieu, a compulsory prelude to the medical studies I had dreamt of since childhood, a choice which thrilled my parents despite their duration and which would require sacrifices from all of us. Having had their fingers burned by law, which was limited by national frontiers, they desired me to enter a profession that could be practised anywhere in the world.

My brother Félix, two years my junior, started the final year of a primary school on our arrival in France: a state school, naturally. At the end of his first school year he obtained his certificate.

It was impossible, because of the lack of money, to send a second child, who dreamed of becoming an architect, to the lycée. He was extremely musical – he played the violin – and good at painting; he drew straight from life. My parents looked for a way to use these artistic gifts. Félix started at a Jewish training school in the rue des Rosiers, to become a jeweller. Apprenticed at Clerc's, near the Opéra, he was boarded at his school but spent every weekend with my parents, while I only saw them during the holidays. Orléans–Paris was a real journey then.

One Sunday evening, following a walk with the family in

the Parc Saint-Cloud, Félix returned to school. The following morning he didn't wake up. After two days in a coma, he died in the main hospital, without my even knowing about it. My parents kept the pain to themselves and left me in Auvergne, where I had been invited to spend my first holiday by the university parish there following my distinction in the first part of my baccalauréat.

Félix is the only member of my family who may perhaps have a tomb in the Jewish cemetery of Thiais, although without any plaque. The marble was probably stolen during the Occupation and on my return I did not have the means to replace it or to extend the concession.

My parents had left Germany only because they did not see any future for their two children and not because they were afraid of dying. Due to my brother's premature death in 1935, I was no longer just the daughter, but also the son, and even the third child they would have liked to have at that moment to fill the horrible void created by the loss of a child who dies before his parents.

We had the status of political refugees and the related work permits. For my parents, certain duties followed from this also. Respectful in particular of their obligation to remain reserved, they stopped being political militants, apart from within the sphere of German emigration. Fortunately, the bulk of this emigration did a lot to inform the French people, thanks mostly to specific organisations such as the Thaelmann Committee. It is no exaggeration to say that we contributed to a correct evaluation of the fascist danger for France during the days of uprising in February 1934 and the bitter fruits of disunity in the German left were a lesson which helped to bring about the victory of the Popular Front.

We could equally foresee that to give back the Ruhr, to allow the re-arming of Germany, not to intervene on the side of the Spanish Republicans against a perjurious and rebellious general, to capitulate at Munich – all this was, in fact, to choose war and Hitler rather than the Popular Front.

But we did not yet know what kind of war lay in wait for us and that it would leave more than 50 million dead.

If I spoke of a second homeland, it is because everything was clear in the minds of my parents as soon as they left Berlin. They would never return to Germany. That country, whose culture they had considered to be their own – my father had published books there to popularise the law – had betrayed them, chased them away, deprived them; they owed nothing to it.

And on 7 January 1937 they got their naturalisation, which included me as a minor. I respected their wishes on my release when I made the same choice for the second time.

So we were French citizens when I began my medical studies. In addition to his legal consultations, my father was dubbing French cinema newsreels into German. My mother had left Nahum Goldmann for the ministry of Georges Mandel, whose offices at 11 rue Tronchet dealt among other things with Alsace using the German language.

We were then on the threshold of this strange war when the French people would be betrayed by those who wanted to take revenge for 1936.

In the first days of September 1939 my father offered himself as a volunteer but the army refused his services, perhaps because he was 48 years old, or perhaps for the same reasons which rapidly and indiscriminately led to the arrest of all the German anti-fascists, Jewish or otherwise, socialists or communists, and to their transfer to internment camps already open for Spanish Republicans.

As French nationals, we avoided the camp at Gurs and were able to show our solidarity with the internees by getting some released, evacuating the children to the country and sending parcels in.

At the time of the military débâcle and the exodus of civilians in May–June 1940, with travel warrants in our pockets and frequently changing trains, the three of us followed the government to Bordeaux. We waited in vain for orders but the German army caught up with us at Bidart, where a summer villa had been requisitioned for us.

It was on that Atlantic beach that the three of us spent our first and last family holiday together since 1933. For a month we deliberated as to what to do, then we returned to Paris. How naive we were!

My father said he had done nothing to be ashamed of. My mother wanted to look for a new job to support us as we were at the end of our small savings. I believed I had an obligation to pursue my medical studies, for which they were ready to make any sacrifice.

It was only after our return home that we learned that the Gestapo had already paid us a visit for a thorough search which had brought no results. Without a doubt our names were on a priority blacklist. And one of my bosses at the Beaujon Hospital had hidden this visit from us so as not to frighten us.

It would have been better to be frightened! Above all, were we not French and protected as such? Not for long!

Today the survivors of my parents' generation, a negligible number – and of mine – very few – have naturally not forgotten (but do the next generations know it, have they learned it?) that under the fascist government of Vichy with the future ex-marshal, the traitor, Philippe Pétain, as head of state, the Jews of France were subjected to a census by green form. It covered the entire country, occupied or not, in order that later the Jews would be decorated with the yellow star, in preparation for the *Shoah*, the so-called Final Solution that Hitler and his acolytes had invented at Wannsee on 20 January 1942. But, ready to go much further than the *Gauleiter* imposed on other occupied countries in Europe, Pétain was to revoke the naturalisations granted in the previous ten years and go for the children.

Our naturalisation, acquired during the Popular Front, did not escape his vigilance. On a day of great sadness I was forced to return our decree of naturalisation to an office of the rue Scribe.

I found it again, carefully filed, several years later. To the civil servant, perhaps the same one, who asked me how it felt to regain my French nationality by means of this document, I remember replying, 'I feel nothing!' It was basically true. A document taken away and then returned did not change anything about my choice or the choice of my parents. But our life would be deeply marked and altered by it.

As soon as the university term began in 1941, I had to interrupt my studies because of a quota system immediately imposed on foreign Jews.

I had finished the third year of my medical studies and I had a passion for pathological anatomy. I owe a lot to the team of laboratory professors who continued to teach me. But one man did even more and remains in my memory for ever: Frédéric Busser, the head of my practical work, took me on as a laboratory assistant and had me give German lessons to his nephew. Through this I also had the good luck to make the acquaintance of Frédéric's father, the great composer and conductor Henri Busser, who died aged 100 well after the war. I have never forgotten his conducting *Pélleas et Mélisande* at the Salle Favart, a beautiful introduction to Debussy, of whom he had been a friend.

I prepared and coloured samples of pathological anatomy all through that year of 1941–42 without knowing that a few months later this knowledge would save my life.

When my comrades in the camp at Auschwitz asked where

to find me after our liberation, I replied automatically, because I didn't know any other reliable address, 'At the laboratory of pathological anatomy at the Paris Medical Faculty'.

Although my father was arrested as a prominent French Jew, by the time of the great round-up my mother and I were stateless.

3 • Drancy

We stayed in the internment camp at Drancy from 16 July to 23 September, rather a long period for foreigners who were only there in transit. They came from Gurs, Pithiviers, Beaune-la-Rolande and other camps where they had been held along with Spanish Republican refugees. They too had had high hopes of France, a land of asylum after the Civil War, which was lost unfairly, due to the path of non-intervention chosen by the French government. The international brigades could not match the strength of the direct support given to the rebels by Hitler and Mussolini. The sky over Guernica remains a witness.

In contrast, it was a short stay compared with those of French origin or the non-denaturalised who managed to remain there, on average, a year longer.

At the time of our transit, the camp was under French administration before passing into the yet more efficient and productive hands of the SS and the Gestapo.

Following a much tried and tested procedure, the 'administrators' had found collaborators among the internees themselves. They knew how to differentiate between a 'Yid' and a French Jew in order to compile, one after the other, the lists of a thousand names for each transportation.

We were difficult to classify, being neither German nor French but assimilated Jews. There was a further reason why our stay lasted more than two months. I was a medical student and the presence of infirmaries immediately pushed me into making myself useful.

The day after our arrival I made myself available to Dr Germain Blechmann, a well-qualified doctor and also a paediatrician who, with two other doctors, Denise Salmon and Michel Elberg, was taking charge of the children's infirmary.

The families of the Vel d'Hiv started to arrive the next day. But our infirmary became mainly a place of welcome for the children who were on their own, whose parents had already been deported and who came to us in small convoys and in a sorry state from Beaune-la-Rolande, Pithiviers and elsewhere.

The big idea was to reunite them with their parents. This fallacious reasoning allowed members of the committee to put their names down on the lists, saying that the Nazis would not harm them and that including a child in a convoy would save the life of an adult.

We did not need to confer on the matter at the children's infirmary. During the short period I was there, we always agreed, from the head of department to the simple medical student, that our duty was to do all we could to save the children.

That means there was never an empty bed in the infirmary. Every child had lice and impetigo at the very least. Many suffered from scabies and infected chicken-pox, the like of which I had never seen and which looked like smallpox, known only to the illustrators of pathology textbooks. Many had measles with side effects which rarely accompany that illness in France. There were more benign illnesses, such as sore throats, but also more serious ones, such as scarlet fever and diphtheria.

We needed the more serious diseases. The risks of contamination, aggravated by promiscuity inside and outside the infirmary, allowed us to prescribe, on account of the danger, the evacuation of sick children to the Claude Bernard and Rothschild Hospitals. Once outside the camp, hope could be reborn.

For this reason we were naturally driven to make false diagnoses, transforming a sore throat into croup, inventing black chicken-pox, making measles pass for scarlet-fever and, in this way, evacuating as many children as possible. I was thrilled at being able to participate in perhaps saving human lives.

But I was unable to save my mother. Even worse, I abandoned her all day long. Remorse torments me even today. I would see her at meals, which I swallowed down quickly, and at night, when I tried to get to sleep by her side on mattresses on the ground, squashed in with other women, with no possibility of privacy.

I know nothing of her thoughts during the weeks before our deportation and I only confided in her in the cattle wagon that carried her to her death.

I do not think she really expected to find my father. Did she regret not having made me flee when those who came to arrest us allowed me to take the attaché, case of family documents downstairs? She never told me. The image I have of my mother in Drancy is one of total despair, of silent resignation, exactly the opposite of the natural vitality and optimism which had made her the true head of the household during our emigration.

In a last exertion, perhaps, of her will to live, she agreed to my giving her injections to bring on a high temperature which might open the doors of Rothschild Hospital to her. The medicines I had access to were not up to the level of my ambition. It is true that, besides a single attack of renal colic, I had never seen my mother ill. The fever took hold of her in the train.

I have yet another aim which preoccupies me prior to leaving in one of those convoys of approximately 1,000 men, women and children which gather in the courtyard several times a week. I am searching for the love I have not yet known. I want to leave as a woman. I am not aware of the fate which awaits pregnant women at the end of their journey.

No problem. The men, some of whom have been here for a year, are greatly in need of both love and sex. It is hardly possible to conduct an affair in the normal way. Furtive caresses during night walks in the yard increase desire. At Drancy, dark corners of staircases are sweet to lovers.

Members of the committee came to warn me and apologise for having listed us for the convoy planned for 23 September. They know that I will not let my mother leave on her own.

But I have not yet decided to let them have their way with me. This new love of mine gives me strength and hope. I drag my mother into the deepest basement of a building. We will not answer to our names at roll call. They will not find us in our dormitory.

All the same, we have prepared the authorised suitcase and taken a blanket. We spend this last night together on the bare ground, huddled together, wrapped in our blanket. In discomfort and insomnia, we begin to talk to one another again.

Is it right to try and escape from our fate and for how long can we get away with it? We are not the first ones to hide. There is always a reserve waiting list. The convoy has to be full. If we do not leave, others, who have not been warned in advance, will take our places. This thought finally becomes unbearable for us.

We were in the yard for the great departure. We did not let our names be called in vain. Colleagues and other friends come to take their leave and wish us a good journey, saying that we will meet again.

Then we are left among the chosen one thousand. Not far from us, I notice a young woman who smiles at me. She was treated at the infirmary for attacks of hysteria, grabbing hold of her bed and refusing to leave. And she is here. She has been given the care of a small child of three. She is now responsible for taking him to his parents.

We are soon at the Gare du Bourget. Our train is composed entirely of cattle wagons, apart from those which carry our guards. We are packed in lots of 50 or more with our luggage and our blankets. Eight horses would be more comfortable. We are speechless with fear; others shriek with terror. Our enemies in uniform shout out their orders. They pass us two buckets full of water. We do not know what awaits us when the folding doors slide shut and we hear the noise of the bar which holds them fast. We are locked in until we reach our destination.

We only have a small rectangle of light and air to watch and breathe through. We have to stretch on tiptoe to stick our heads out. The opening is too small to escape through, maybe a child … but there aren't any in our group.

The luggage is in our way and deprives us of a lot of space but each of us hangs on to the last belongings we have left. Little by little life gets organised. When the first bucket of water has been drunk, it becomes a toilet. Blankets are stretched out to curtain off a corner. When the bucket is full, urine and faeces are evacuated, as well as can be, on to the railway line by the only available opening. A nauseating smell travels with us.

We organise ourselves to take turns to stand next to the opening, to escape the smell for a short while. Those who stand there tell us which stations we are passing. Most of the stops are deep in the countryside. We are not a priority train. We see ordinary passenger trains passing, we shout, most people avoid lifting their heads. Some have a look full of pity.

What we need is help, but there is no hope. We know that we are going eastwards. As we pass from time to time railwaymen working on the lines, I have the idea of preparing paper notes with a message and address and throwing them out. We also stop in the Gare de Metz, next to a passenger train with a compartment full of nuns. They see my note fall. Most of these messages reached their destination, but I did not find any messages for me when I returned. No one was waiting for me.

During this long journey, in unbearable conditions, my mother and I were together for the last time. My head resting often in her lap, I told her about my first love affair. I told her I was certain that this war would soon be over with a final victory over fascism. I promised that on our return to France I would finish my medical studies, and that she would not have to worry about anything.

My mother kissed me a lot and said nothing. Her eyes were extremely sad. I believe she was thinking of my brother, who had escaped this catastrophe by a premature death, and of my father whom she hoped to see again.

She probably felt more than I did the transformation which had occurred in me after the few weeks I spent in Drancy. She forgave me for having neglected her and having become an independent woman and an adult. I never forgave myself for it; I still carry the burden today.

Having left at dawn on 23 September 1942,[*] we reached our destination on the 25th in the evening. That day my mother was 50 years old. I wished her, with optimism, many happy returns on her last birthday.

---

[*]See Serge Klarsfeld, *Le Mémorial de la déportation des juifs de France. Convoi no. 36.*

4 · Birkenau

After a violent halt there is silence first, our anxious silence, questioning. What next? We are at the end of the world.

Orders are yelled at us in German. We hear the bars that have kept us prisoner for three days being raised. The doors are opened with a shattering noise. We sigh with relief. It is not a station, but our terminus. Our eyes have difficulty getting used to the semi-darkness which surrounds us.

'Raus', 'runter', 'schnell', 'schneller' (Out, down, fast, faster). We jump down from our wagons, our suitcases and pathetic bundles in our hands. I remember a waste-ground where the rails end sharply. We wait on a sort of slope.

Orders come thick and fast: 'Alles liegen lassen'. (Drop everything!) We drop our last luggage. 'Vorwärts'. (Move forward!) We move forward. Someone grabs our handbags; we don't even see who it is. I take my mother's hand, we look at each other. In her eyes is an unspeakable suffering. She mutters to me: 'We have no identity left, we are nobody!'

There are a thousand of us and we jostle one another as we march to our first selection. A voice that orders, shouts: Männer rechts, Frauen links.' We don't need a translation, but we tell those around us that men and women have to separate here. It is the women who hold the children by the hand.

Two columns are formed in a disorderly fashion. It gets difficult to move forward. We reach a line of lorries where we are divided again.

Men in uniform push the women and children towards the lorries. I notice for the last time the young woman from the infirmary holding the hand of the child she's been put in charge of. They also direct towards the lorries the disabled, the sick and 'the old'.

My mother is 50 years old today and will always remain that age. She clings on to my arm when they try to separate her from me. We reach the SS commander. She addresses him in German: 'Lassen Sie mich mit meiner Tochter gehen, ich kann gut laufen'. ('Let me go with my daughter. I am a good walker.') It is true that she has always been an excellent walker, better than I. And the *Kommandant* – I learned soon after that he was called Aumeier and was hanged in Poland after a trial following liberation – answers her with exquisite politeness: 'Machen Sie sich keine Sorgen, gnädige Frau, wir wollen Ihnen den Weg erleichtern. Sie finden Ihre Tochter im Lager wieder.' ('Don't worry, Madam, we want to make your journey easier for you. You will find your daughter again in the camp.')

My mother lets go of me. We look at each other intently, profoundly, silently. We are separated and I don't see her climb into the lorry. We did not say goodbye to each other. We did not kiss. I never saw my mother again!

We are grouped into rows of five and counted; 126 of us women enter Birkenau camp on foot. We hardly notice the entrance gate. As we go up inside the camp, weird shadows spin around us. They remind me of the witches of my childhood fairy tales. But these pitiful ghosts are the inhabitants of this place. What do they want from us? Voices whisper to us to give them what we still possess, tell us that we will be left with nothing. I still have my watch on my wrist: I don't want to lose my awareness of time. I pay no attention to these agitated voices.

We reach a building at the other end of the camp, the only one lit in the night to welcome us. We go inside and soon learn that this is the *Sauna*; later on we will learn that this is a cynical trick.

We quickly discover that we are to spend what remains of the night here. A few groups form and discuss their apprehension in low voices.

At last a voice is raised above the others in German. It is a woman in striped clothes, grey and blue, with an armband on which is written the word *Kapo* (Chief of *Kommando*, foreman, generally auxiliary to the SS). She clarifies matters with brutality and frankness.

We are now *Häftlinge* (prisoners, detainees) and, once the admission formalities are completed, we will be allocated to a *Block* in the camp for the nights and to one of the commandos during the day for work.

We want to know when the lorries with our relatives will arrive. They should have preceded us. Then we learn the horrible truth, which no one was prepared for. These lorries will not enter the camp; they have another destination. 'You will never see the people who got into them again. They have gone straight to the gas chambers.'

I understand instantly the fate reserved for my mother and my tears dry up for the whole period of my detention. You cannot weep in the midst of barbarism.

I do my best to translate the information for the women who don't understand German. Then I approach the *Kapo* to learn more. I speak to her using the polite form of address and she laughs in my face. Here the familiar form of address has to be used among co-detainees.

I want to know whether my mother will suffer. She does not think so. There is a whole drama put on to hide their imminent death. They will believe they are going into a sauna for a shower. They will undress and be entitled to a towel and soap. After that, she does not know exactly how things will proceed in detail but she thinks it will be a quick death.

I learnt much later that this wasn't so. Zyklon B certainly kills, but starting from ground level. The *Sonderkommando*, responsible for the evacuation of the gas chambers and the removal of corpses to crematory ovens, discovered human pyramids. The dead at the bottom had succumbed first; the others, more resilient and stronger, had tried to hoist themselves up to the top where it was still possible to breathe. The last to succumb, after interminable minutes, would be right at the top.

We are hungry, we are tired. We have to sit on the ground, or, better still, lie down, to doze off. So many hours pass by in this manner that I stop looking at my watch. Here time has no meaning.

Some time during the night or at day-break a voice shakes us out of our lethargy: 'Aufstehen' (Get up). It is time for our first meal in the camp. We have our first soup out of large dark-red metallic bowls; it is the best soup I can remember. It is thick and tastes of dry beans. I see some of my comrades unable to swallow this purée. They wait for what is to follow; nothing follows.

From that first meal I decide I will not push aside anything which is edible. My parents trained me to be able to eat anything. As a child I spent hours sitting at meals I didn't like. Either I forced myself to eat or I found the same meal heated up in the evening. But countless other comrades refuse to eat the disgusting camp food from the very first day and consciously or unconsciously contribute to their own deaths. The food rations are calculated in such a way that malnutrition brings death after about six months. And we are not yet aware of the other ways of dying quicker than that.

Scarcely have we finished this meal then our *Sauna* is invaded by men and women in stripes and men and women in SS uniform.

We learn the names of the commandos who register the survivors of our convoy: '*Schreibstube*' (registration bureau), '*Politische Abteilung*' (political section). We realise at the same time that the men are elsewhere, at Auschwitz.

We have to declare our identity, origin, nationality, profession. I tell the truth as if through this registration I am
reclaiming my individuality. I know that others lied and they
were right to do so. There are no documents to prove
anything to the contrary. They have taken the first step in
their struggle for survival. Some are no longer Jewish; others
change their names and their professions.

After registration, in another corner of the building, we are
made to undress. There are women but also men, with and
without uniform. I do so quickly; others drag on, ashamed.
The process of degradation has begun.

The commando *'Friseur'* (hairdresser) moves into action.
Our hair soon piles up on the floor, straight and curly, dark
and blonde, in a multi-coloured carpet. They shave our heads,
our armpits, our pubises. For hygienic reasons, it seems, not a
single hair must remain. We hardly recognise one another any
more. We try to joke about it, saying 'This close shave suits
me'. I look like a chubby baby, known as 'Baby Cadum', an
advertisement utterly superfluous in this place.

Then we are taken to the cloakroom to get dressed again.
Naturally, we don't put our own clothes back on. They are
judged to be dirty and taken for fumigation before being used
for others.

As Jewish women, except for those who managed to claim
there has been an error and keep their hair, we are not entitled
to the striped clothes reserved for Aryan women. We have no
choice either among the heap of dirty but disinfected clothes
ready for us. We must accept what the *'Kleidungskammer'*
(wardrobe) commando offers us. There are knickers with
traces of menstrual blood, dresses too long or too short,
summer or winter clothes. These dresses, in order not to
remain civilian clothing but to become outfits for Jewish
deportees, are daubed down the back with a wide vertical line
of red paint.

I am lucky: the clothes I inherit are rather clean and just

about fit me. I get a brown autumn dress and I am not going to suffer from the cold straight away.

But on this 26 September I am going to have another stroke of luck. On that day we are allowed to keep our own shoes. In the middle of July, at the time of our arrest, I made a curious choice. I hated those shoes with a wooden sole, which had become fashionable through sheer hardship, and I took my mountain shoes, high-buttoned and all leather, comfortable to wear. Being able to keep them makes me feel comfortable, even without socks. I kept those shoes almost until the end and they saved my life, but I do not know this yet. We have to walk a lot and often to run to survive.

Dressed again, we go back to the registration table where the 'tattooers' are waiting for us. The great speciality of Auschwitz, our number, so it is indelible, must be marked in the flesh of our left forearm. I happen on a Berlin woman who, to oblige a 'compatriot', tries to embroider me a pretty number. I become number 20832 until the end of my days.

Then our Stars of David are distributed to us: half yellow, half red, with an F for France and a band of white material to be marked with the new number. The whole thing is to be stitched on the left breast of our dresses.

All these initiation ceremonies take a whole day of our lives, a day unforgettable for the survivors. Auschwitz is tattooed into our bodies.

The process of degradation is put into gear. We are no longer individuals, we are numbers. We are still human beings that a skillful organisation is going to try and transform into beasts.

We are now ready to be incorporated into the life of Birkenau, the Birch Meadow, this pretty name given to the worst of the camps of the Final Solution invented for the Jews.

An *Aufseherin* – we have learned this word for the SS women in charge of guarding us – makes us leave the *Block Sauna*, where, at the end of the day, we did not even have the right to have a quick wash.

She directs us to a *Block* on the other side of the camp, almost opposite. Roll call in front of the other *Blöcke* started long ago. Grouped apart – we have already been counted and recounted – we watch how things will be for us from tomorrow onwards.

There is almost no movement in the camp. In front of the *Blöcke* long queues of women stand stock still in rows of five. Here and there detainees with the armband *Läuferin* (runner) run to centralise the results. It always takes hours to get the correct count. It is the *Aufseherinnen*, assisted by the *Blockältesten* (block senior) and the *Stubendienst* (barracks cleaning duty), who watch out for order and silence in the ranks.

The dead are also part of the roll call. The morning call includes women who died in the night and who are fetched from their *Koje* (three-tiered sleeping niche) to be lined up on the ground next to their comrades. At evening roll call, they count the women who died at work and whom the external commandos have to bring back. After the call, the *Leichenkommando* (corpse commando) begins the process of piling up the corpses, instead of their being collected by the *Sonderkommando*.

Perhaps we didn't know or understand all this the first evening, but to remain alive we have to understand as quickly as possible. And life is short.

After roll call, most women rush to their *Blöcke*; others walk around. We new arrivals see some *Kapos* approaching us wanting to recruit our fresh blood for their next-day commandos. They have had some deaths. Some sick people will go to the *Revier* (sick bay). We must at all costs have a full workforce this evening to prevent delay tomorrow. A process of bidding to present the proposed commando in the best light takes place. As one has to work – it is prohibited to remain in the camp without a valid reason – most women from my convoy let themselves be enrolled straight away to make sure they get a good job. Of course they cannot know that three weeks after our arrival they will all be dead.

I have another idea. I was able to make myself useful at the Drancy infirmary. Here too, there must be infirmaries to treat the sick. I already know who among us are doctors, midwives and nurses. Like the *Kapos*, I scour our ranks to recruit all who are likely to be useful to our sick, rather than let them be recruited to serve our enemies. Twelve of us agree with my proposal to offer our services to the camp health authorities tomorrow morning.

Our soup arrives. The *Blockova* took some of us to carry the heavy *Kübel* (large metal containers, already heavy when empty) to our group from the nearby kitchen. There's pushing and shoving. Hunger has been at us for a long time. We are first given a large red bowl and a spoon each. The veterans who surround us advise us to look after them as if they were the apple of our eye.

They tell us to queue up in single file to be served. Then an unexpected phenomenon takes place. It is no longer pushing and shoving; an actual battle breaks out between a number of women to get to the front of the queue, where I find myself by chance. I have no wish to fight to keep my place. I leave the queue and sit on the ground. It is a painful scene. It ends with truncheon blows from a *Stubova* who manages to get everyone back into line. The strongest have pushed to the front. They don't know that whatever is the thickest part of the soup remains at the bottom. For a fair distribution the soup has to be stirred constantly, which is too tiring, and that evening the last are better served than the first.

So I saw that we can fight each other, that our civilisation is just a gloss which is easy to rub off. We will have to struggle against our basic instincts if we want to remain human and not devour each other like beasts.

To fight and be beaten with batons is part of the programme designed for our annihilation. I decide that day that I will never fight to eat, that I will never lift a hand to beat anyone.

With this deliberate choice I have put, without realising it, a third piece of luck on my side. I am no longer alone, I have many comrades.

Night has already fallen when we are ushered into our housing *Block*. The *Blockova* shouts at us to find sleeping places, but otherwise doesn't bother about us.

The *Block* is organised into *Koje*, a kind of niche on three levels. The best places are on the top level. On the others it is impossible to sit up. The most exhausted of us collapse at the bottom.

A few of us together manage to lift ourselves towards a gap in the middle. Under us there are straw mattresses; in these mattresses there are fleas. They dance wildly over our ravaged bodies. In the morning we discover a rash of small red stings all over our skin. We have not yet learned how to live with vermin.

During the night I feel myself getting soaked with a warm liquid. Urine runs down on me from the floor above. I was horrified and furious to observe such a lack of restraint. Why not have the courage to get up and go to the toilet? Soon I will learn that going to the 'bog' can cost one's life and that urine, which is pleasantly warm in winter, is also our best antiseptic.

The sun has not yet risen and we have barely slept when the words 'roll call' echo around. We have to get outside quickly. *Blockälteste* and *Stubendienst* are allowed batons. We saw the day before that they know how to use them and what we must do to avoid them. We get into lines. The *Blockälteste* counts us before the arrival of the SS *Aufseherin*. The *Stubendienst* checks no one is hiding in the *Block*. Our SS arrives, the *Blockälteste* presents the workforce, the other one counts us. With a bit of luck the count is right first time. But we have to stand until it is over.

We are not as still during the roll calls as I thought when I watched it at first. To combat the cold, we will learn how to stamp our feet. We will struggle against the numbness of our bodies by holding our elbows and swaying our silhouettes in a regular rhythm. It is the ebb and flow of a human sea.

Roll call is over, which means that the number of available workers from our *Block* has been taken to the gate for confirmation, compared with the other *Blöcke*, and added up to give the SS administration of the camp the exact daily number of detainees. The *Schreibstube* keeps our register from day to day.

The transports that come in gradually replace the dead. But when there are too many they don't even come into the camp; they are not registered or tattooed. They go straight to the gas chamber. Entire convoys disappeared into it.

After roll call, they pour a hot beverage into our bowls. It's a kind of herbal tea that we will call *tchaï* or *herbata*. Obviously we need to drink, but some of it will be used to wash a little.

There are water taps for washing in the camp and also a communal toilet. We sit there side by side and back to back to relieve ourselves in the large gap in the middle, into which there is a risk of slipping if alone and too emaciated or too weak. We will find out how dangerous, even fatal, this place is at night.

Then comes the distribution of foodstuffs for the day. We get a piece of bread with a thin layer of margarine. It is difficult not to eat it all straight away. We are hungry and we have nowhere to store our treasures. We are already hampered by our bowls and spoons and we guess that without these utensils there won't be any soup in the evening.

We rapidly become aware of our daily menu. In the morning tea, or rather an infusion of unknown herbs, undrinkable. To take to work, a piece of bread, about 100 grammes in weight, of the type of dark-brown bread which keeps endlessly and which we will cut into five to ration ourselves. It is served alternately with a scraping of margarine, a slice of sausage or a spoonful of jam made with saccharin. Then, after evening roll call, soup, rarely hot, with pieces of swede and potato peelings floating in it, the rest unidentifiable. The soup is never thick and cannot satisfy our hunger or fill our stomachs.

The senior staff of the *Block* serve themselves first in the afternoon, as soon as they have fetched the *Kübel*. They fish around to get the solid bits. Tiny pieces of meat or bacon fat and recognisable vegetables. I only get to taste these at a much later stage.

Later on, when practising my future profession of doctor, I became interested in food hygiene and nutrition. I estimated our daily camp ration at about 600–800 calories.

It is not surprising to discover rapidly that we are surrounded by walking skeletons with prominent bellies. At that boundary between life and imminent death they are known as 'Muslims'. I never knew how or why this word entered the concentration camp vocabulary.

After morning roll call, during which we see night give way to day, the commandos are formed. The *Kapos* run everywhere, working to gather up the required number of workers. Those who run into trouble drag along even detainees who are visibly ill or exhausted. After all, to die in the camp or at work comes to the same. In fact it is dangerous to stay behind; death lies in wait much more on the spot than outside.

Meanwhile I collect my little group together. When the columns start moving we overtake them to go and present our request at the gate. Those who pass the gate can read day after day *'Arbeit macht frei'* (Work brings freedom). For us this freedom is a programmed death. I do not remember the details of the discussion I had with the SS officer on duty, supervising the commandos leaving. We look healthy, we are French, even if, being Jewish women, we have shaven heads and, according to my explanation, we are competent. He has, in any case, the necessary authority to take us to the camp doctor who says 'yes' and we are immediately allocated to the three existing *Reviere, Blöcke* 22, 23 and 24.

With Sonia from Paris, Esther from Poitiers and another comrade whose name I have forgotten, we head for *Block* 24. It is the *Revier* for sick German women, Aryans and *Reichsdeutsche* ('pure' Germans). We have been posted there because we are judged the best qualified and because I speak fluent German. The *Blockälteste* who admits us is called Klara and wears a 'civil rights' green triangle. She explains at once that she is a midwife, condemned for being a 'maker of angels' (i.e. abortions).

Four more comrades are posted to *Block* 22, which is reserved for the other Aryans, mainly the *Volksdeutsche* and Polish women.

The last four, the unlucky ones, led by Markus, a tall, attractive and strong midwife, go to *Block* 23, the Jewish *Revier*. We will only ever see them again for a short while.

It is my third piece of luck that I start my life at Birkenau with this work in the German *Revier*. I even get a supplementary piece of luck. At the end of the *Revier*, separated from the patients by curtains, there are bedsteads, one on top of the other, made of wood, reserved for the nursing staff. Two are free. Sonia is a doctor, Klara offers her one of them. As in her eyes I am almost a doctor, she offers me the other one. I glance at our two comrades, who will have to return and sleep in the *Block* where we came from. I suggest to Klara that I share my bed with Esther; she agrees. Sonia appears absent-minded and does not pick up my idea for herself.

A week later our fourth comrade, forced to join the roll calls outside her *Block*, ended her life by grabbing the electrified barbed wire that surrounds the camp. She had the good fortune to die straight away, which was not always the case. In spite of her privileged work during the day, she couldn't bear the prolonged standing at the endless roll calls.

Esther and I sleep head to toe in our wooden bedstead, a straw mattress underneath, a blanket on top. We are a team.

The roll call with the reduced workforce from our *Block* is a formality and over soon. Our patients are Aryan German women. We have to nurse them properly and cure them. They are not systematically condemned to the Final Solution. Some have hope and will be released once their prison terms are completed.

Our working tools are non-existent. I have one thermometer for 25 patients and one water bottle to collect water for washing them. Klara explains that we have three diagnoses to enter on our forms: fever, diarrhoea and sores. These symptoms correspond to our three means of therapy: aspirin, tannin and coal, and rolls of crêpe paper.

We soon understand that the real diagnosis is reserved for the SS doctor on his round. He alone decides other treatments.

It is obvious that no one comes to the *Revier* with a cold, flu or toothache. Women who have fever and coughs suffer from tuberculosis; those who have higher fever and spots on their bodies have eruptive typhus (spread by lice); and those who have diarrhoea have amoebic or bacillic dysentery, or even cholera. Those who have sores suffer from vitamin deficiency or serious burns after having failed to commit suicide on the high-voltage electric fences.

Those who cannot hold it in have worms in their straw mattresses and on their sores. Cleaning and bandaging with crepe paper is useless.

We also have to collect soup for our patients from the kitchen at the other end of the camp. This gives us a chance to get some fresh air but the full *Kübel* is too heavy for two to carry. Esther and I are well organised; being two together is a strength in itself. Sonia, who is rather haughty, keeps to herself and shares nothing.

Every evening after roll call we try to make contact with the comrades from our convoy. Each day we learn of new disappearances. Those in the greatest hurry commit suicide. Once up on the electrified perimeter fence, the final blissful shock can shoot out from the nearest observation point. Those less courageous go to *Block* 25, which is behind the Jewish *Revier*.

Block 25 is the ante-room of the gas-chamber. This fact is learned very quickly. It is possible to go there spontaneously, to choose this type of death. No more distribution of food there; it would be a waste on the part of the SS camp management. But one can have a rest before dying. A girl of my age followed her mother there. Her mother was the same age as mine.

I am convinced that I wouldn't have returned from deportation if my mother had come to the camp. I wouldn't have been able to bear seeing her deteriorate and die. My love for her would have taken away all my strength; I would have followed her. That too is one of my pieces of luck.

In my memory I still see my father and mother as living people. Both will remain alive until I myself die.

Not everyone in *Block* 25 is a volunteer. The SS with the help of the *Kapos* throw the weak in there, the women who are completely exhausted and refuse to go to work, or those who on return from work don't run fast enough to reach their *Block*. This is called 'selection' and generally only concerns the Jewish women. The game these hunters stalk has shaven skulls.

When there are enough people in *Block* 25, a tarpaulin-covered lorry comes along and collects its cargo for delivery to the gas chamber.

There is a space in front of our *Revier*. The lorry stops there, sometimes even while we are outside for roll call. Our comrades are brought in like a docile herd. They climb up, helping each other, or are pushed in one after the other. Occasionally a final burst of energy, a final revolt in the face of death pushes a victim to break ranks and escape. The chase begins but the race is unequal and the result fatal. The lorry leaves with its full cargo.

It even happens that at the last minute, seized by the urge to kill, an SS or an *Aufseherin* pounces on an extra victim and she then joins this last journey. It is useless trying to jump off the lorry as it is always surrounded by soldiers and dogs.

Three weeks later we no longer find any faces we recognise in our first *Block*, so we stop going there. We maintain daily contact with the other *Reviere*. It is easy to keep in touch with our neighbour, *Block* 22, where the treatment is already a bit less caring for the ordinary *Volksdeutsche* than for those in our *Block*.

The Jewish *Revier* is further away and almost a prohibited zone. We have to wait for our comrade Markus to get out of it for a few minutes. We learn from her that the Jewish *Revier* must be avoided as it is difficult to leave it other than horizontally.

Selections are made daily by SS doctor Clauberg. Perhaps he disagrees with industrial death by gas chamber. He prefers to kill the victims of his choice individually and scientifically.

Our friend tells us that Clauberg makes her hold people's

arms for intravenous injections which have an immediate effect. She does not know what substance it is; maybe it is simply air to provoke gaseous embolisms. She tells us she won't be able to bear it much longer. Soon after we stop seeing her, victim in her turn of an injection or a selection.

The patient in my *Block* 24 whom I remember best is a Jehovah's Witness. I had never heard of this religious sect before. At that time they were being deported for refusing to take part in the war effort, including the women who refused to do related service. They are, therefore, German. The most courageous carry on their opposition even in the camp, refusing to leave with the external commandos. I saw them on their knees, praying together after roll call.

My patient is severely burned after an attempt at electrified suicide, although it is against her religion. Her wounds feed an army of worms. My treatment could not save her.

Later I observe that the SS have found a solution for the less fussy 'Witnesses'. They become 'general-purpose maids' for the SS families installed with wives and children in the villas close to the camp.

'One louse and you die!', proclaim the health posters in the camp. It is true, by means of typhus or selection, but nothing can be done with these parasites in the everyday unhygienic conditions imposed in the concentration camps, particularly Birkenau. I discover this quickly.

First of all I see my comrades at roll-call time searching their necklines and catching something which they crush between their finger-nails. I see scenes that remind me of those amusing monkeys on the rocks of Vincennes. Here it shocks me, until I start to have my own itchings.

In my third-year medicine class I got a good mark in parasitology. I loved working with a microscope. Naturally I was familiar with the louse's monstrous head. A few summers earlier when I had helped the mother of a 'poor family' in Normandy, I caught some in my hair. The Marie-Rose[*] soon got rid of them. But with the body lice of Birkenau, you need to wage a tireless daily battle. Most of the time it is they who win and we who die.

My fifth piece of luck is surviving typhus and, what is more, at the Jewish *Revier*. As far as I can recall the twelve women who survived from my convoy by working in the *Reviere* all contracted typhus, one after the other, around the fifth week after our arrival, at the beginning of November.

When Esther and I start to develop a fever, we decide to stay on our feet as long as possible and to carry on working as if nothing has happened. We want to stay away from the Jewish *Revier* and its deadly risks.

Thanks to my thermometer, we know that our temperatures fluctuate around 40°C. We manage to resist for several days. The hardest thing is crossing the camp to fetch the soup from the kitchen. We manage to keep our balance by hanging on to our *Kübel* but it becomes far too heavy. We are growing weaker. So one day by mutual agreement we gave in.

Dying for the sake of dying, we might as well die lying down, without further exertion. Arm in arm, to support one another, we said our goodbyes to Klara, who had treated us well, and whom we never saw again. Then we left for the other side of the camp, and went into our *Revier* 23, near *Block* 25, the ante-room of death.

We are put in a *Koje* on the top level; Dorka is already there. Through our tiny window we can see those who are going to die, those for whom the choice has already been made.

When I lie on my back I feel dizzy and everything turns around me. During these dizzy spells I cling to my precious shoes, which I have put under my head so they won't be stolen.

A few memories emerge from my illness. Close by, in

*Trademark of a powder used at the time to combat lice.

a middle *Koje*, Sonia, who entered the *Revier* before us, is delirious. Every day she declares that the Americans have disembarked and that her boyfriend Hervé is coming to fetch her. For her, victory has come and she dies smiling at him several days later. Dorka dies too, of a sore throat which nobody bothers to nurse. It's pointless making a diagnosis. Our problem is to live or die. Medical care is practically non-existent.

Dorka's corpse remains at our side for several days. Finally our yelling is loud enough again to be heard. They take the body away.

Being among ourselves, all Jewish women, our food rations are correctly distributed. But we're not hungry. We eat our soup and trade on the black market with our bread. We're not the only ones to take advantage of our fever. It is known outside. Every night, around the *Revier* revolve shadows who, during their day at work, have succeeded in 'organising' something more precious for us than our bread: a carrot, an onion, in other words vitamins.

The word 'organise' enters my concentration-camp vocabulary in place of the word 'steal'. You do not 'steal' from the SS. What you organise can be traded, hence the existence of the night market in the camp.

When I get better, I 'organise' myself a pullover. We are starting to feel the cold in spite of each having a blanket. Winter is almost here and I have nothing but a dress. One morning I spot in a neighbouring passage a comrade who has died in the night; she is in a lower *Koje* of which I have a bird's-eye view. I am obviously the first to notice it and must move fast. I get down surreptitiously to grab the pullover of the dead woman without hesitation or shame; she no longer needs it. You cannot rob the dead either.

Back next to Esther, I examine my catch. It seems to be alive: lice are running everywhere. Having resisted typhus, I only fear the bites, but all the same it is disgusting and I devote myself for hours on end to a laborious delousing, crushing louse after louse between my nails. Then I slip on this first warm piece of clothing.

I also saw a selection inside *Block* 23. One morning, after roll call, they count us in our *Kojes*. Our *Stubendienst* gets busy, tidies, cleans up. I understand we are going to be blessed with a visit from Clauberg, the SS doctor-in-chief, in person. He too was hanged after a trial in Poland, while Mengele managed to escape the justice of men, though not the judgement of history.

Shortly after the 'Achtung!' (Attention) of the *Blockova*, the hated uniforms invade. The highest rank does not wear a white coat but holds a riding whip. It is with this that he is going to clear places for new patients. No need to burden oneself with diagnoses. His steely eyes decide who is going to die and who has a chance of living a bit longer.

All the women he strikes with his whip are pulled down from their straw mattresses by his acolytes. Some stay standing up, trembling; others collapse on the ground, unable to get up. Then the expulsion starts with fresh lashes of the whip accompanied by baton blows from the *Aufseherin* and the other SS, who revel in the show.

Block 25 is just behind; the journey for the human cattle won't take long. Those who refuse to walk or cannot are dragged outside by the *Stubendienst* and go on being brutally beaten.

We see our comrades climb or be lifted into the lorry which is waiting for them. Then those who had been temporarily reprieved in *Block* 25 come out to complete the cargo. Well-packed, one against the other, there is not enough room for everyone. A few 'Muslims' are forced back into their *Block*. They are for the next time; the gas chambers are there but they can wait.

Esther and I are not going to wait. The murdering whirlwind

39

may return tomorrow. We decide to quit the *Revier* immediately.

Permission granted. Others, more or less cured, often very weak, react like us. It is not the fear of dying but the will to live that pushes us outside.

We try to go back to *Revier* 24 to resume our work. It is impossible even to get close. Our places have been taken. Klara has been released.

The only solution left is to be accepted into another *Block* and to look for an outside work commando for the following day.

Nearby we catch the *Blockova* of *Block* 26 unawares, admiring her war treasure of jewels and gold. Yes, it is possible to organise gold, precious stones, silver from all countries, because the deportees bring all kinds of things straight to the fertile belly of the foul beast. The SS who manage the concentration camp are fabulously rich in booty of all sorts. She will be able to buy the favours of an SS, or be hanged, which will happen to her later on. Meanwhile she is in a good mood and accedes to our request by offering us the top part of a *Koje*, close to her and where there is even a blanket.

It is a considerable piece of luck which we will defend every night. When, after roll call, everyone rushes inside, the fight for places and blankets begins. Thanks to our speed and our proximity to the *Blockova*, who has a soft spot for us (maybe because we share her secret), we manage to keep the place and the blanket.

The most important thing is to be taken on and leave for work the following day. Esther and I share between us the job of sounding out different *Blöcke*, where we question our comrades about their commandos and *Kapos*.

I hear of a commando where the work is a long walk away. Good shoes and sufficient strength are needed. Because of this, this commando faces daily defections and we have a good chance of being welcome. Esther agrees. Walking, provided we can stand the strain, can be less hard than working.

The next day after roll call we have no problem getting on to that commando. Once we have passed the gate, we feel we are breathing better. It is the first time we've left the precinct since our arrival. The weather is fine and all the time we belong to this commando we walk beneath radiant sunshine, not uncommon in November. I recall an endless horizon beyond the barbed wire of the camp. I see once again roads, fields and especially trees. These leafless trees are covered with white morning frost. They look as if they have been cut by a master glazier and reflect the sunlight with all the colours of the rainbow.

For the first time in weeks, I communicate with nature and feel reassured. Beauty is a sign of life; I feel stronger. We lost our concept of time long ago. I think our march lasts about two hours, and no doubt a bit more on the way back. We never met a living soul on this path, which finally leads to a kind of immense hangar filled with sand.

I don't know why we are doing this work. This sand that is moved away may be used to put out fires, build something, we don't care. We only care about saving our strength.

While the *Ober-* and *Unter-Kapos*, (yes, there are grades!) chat, or even flirt, with our warders, and the dogs are resting, we have to shovel. We spread out from the back of the hangar up to the entrance and shovel out the sand in an unbroken rhythm.

I quickly learn to work slowly, to do the least possible in order to keep going. It is relatively easy; our guards hardly watch us. Yet we do have to keep a constant eye on them and shovel hard when they glance at us. We keep watch on them in turn while some shift their loads of sand and others rest on the handles of their shovels.

I remember a slice of lemon I unearthed with my shovel. I swallowed it, sand and all, for the few vitamins it might still contain.

Including the return journey, our working day is shortened by about four hours, which is very much appreciated. Furthermore the walk warms up our feet. So when we need to run to escape from the evening selection, once we have passed the gate we charge in a zigzag towards our *Block* 26. We run past a comrade who like us left the Jewish *Revier* the day before. With her wooden-soled sandals, she is bogged down in the mud of the camp. She won't get out of it. Cured the day before, she is condemned to die the following one.

At our place of work we cannot 'organise' anything, not even along the journey. At the camp black market the only thing we have to exchange is our food rations, which are already insufficient to keep us alive. Yet I give half of my bread ration to Esther who needs to smoke. For a full ration of bread we get three cigarettes; they belonged to a woman who was condemned to death.

At night, having victoriously defended our blanket, we find it difficult, in spite of our tiredness, to get to sleep. The itching provoked by lice bites gives us no respite. We scratch each other's backs, taking care not to tear the skin which could lead to infection. With the accumulated fatigue we sleep a little, one night in two. When sleepless we pursue our lice-hunting vigorously. We function almost like monkeys: one movement, one louse caught. But we don't bite them between our teeth: our nails suffice to crush them.

So we can keep a better watch on the surrounding area, we try to go together to the 'collective latrine', which has no water. We soon give up the idea out of fear and weakness. It is not safe to walk about the camp in the middle of the night. You can come across a night patrol, be attacked and end up in *Block* 25.

We decide, therefore, to convert one of our mess bowls into a chamber pot and put it in a corner of our *Koje*. From that time on, we eat our soup out of the same bowl. The concern about hygiene we retain makes us take great care not to mix up the two bowls.

I learn at this time that saliva is a good antiseptic and can replace alcoholic solution. I treat two whitlows, one on each hand, by constantly keeping the two damaged fingers in the moisture of my mouth. Discreetly, I also let urine run down my legs whenever possible. I hope to avoid infecting my sores.

There is always a great rush when, in the early morning, we are chased by whistle blows and shouts to line up for roll call in front of our *Block*. In this race, Esther and I pass a *Koje* where two girls 'from Canada' sleep in the middle floor. This special commando is made up of beautiful girls that the SS, nicknamed 'der schöne Fritz' (the handsome Fritz), chooses himself. I never met him, but he has the reputation of wanting to surround his virile good looks with the female beauties that come into the camp. He has to select them as soon as they arrive because our beauty is perishable.

This commando is in charge of sorting out the belongings we drop after we get off the train. It is a privileged commando because Fritz wants his girls to remain beautiful. They handle riches and, when he chooses to, Fritz closes his eyes.

Naturally these detainees 'organise' first what they need to dress themselves up in, but they don't find anything to eat in what they sort out. They will strive to bring into the camp anything that can be traded for food; like us, they eat the normal food of the camp.

That is how cigarettes, gold, jewels get in, things that can only be traded with the *Blockovas, Stubendienst, Kapos* and other staff detainees who collaborate with the SS to preserve the internal and external order of the camp. For black market exchanges they bring in more precious articles: combs, toothbrushes, lingerie, clothes. All these things must be smuggled in for there are, of course, searches at the entrance to the camp. Being caught means being hanged. But death can also come from simple exclusion from the 'Canada' commando or direct selection to *Block* 25. It is Fritz who decides and, oddly, he sometimes forgives and forgets or even defends his girls. If I mention all this, it is to say that the girls 'from Canada' are rich but they run the same risks as the rest of us.

One morning I see on their floor some gloves of which I am in great need. I grab them while running for roll call. It is a second-degree organisation of which I am not ashamed, because in 'Canada' it is possible to replace these gloves the same day. For me, they are a vital necessity as the cold is getting worse and worse. Frostbites turn into sores and these become infected.

Comb, toothbrush, knickers, brassiere, woollens: I had to go without food to acquire them.

Most of us in the camp are fortunate enough not to have our periods any longer. I thought for a long time that we were drugged to achieve this result. I no longer think so. We simply stopped menstruating naturally, because of the dreadful life we lead.

Even more unbearable than hunger is thirst. Apart from the horrible morning infusion and the evening watery soup, there is nothing. Our bodies become unavoidably dehydrated. In this context the problem of drinking water no longer bothers me. I suck the icicles which are formed on the roofs of our *Blöcke* and elsewhere. I break the ice of puddles I come across on the road.

The punishment is diarrhoea. It strikes us down and we cannot resist. 'Hose runter, Hose rauf! (Knickers down, knickers up): we repeat the joke endlessly.

There are no toilets and even less toilet paper. I still suffer from this obsession. Even today I feel sick at the idea of having no paper.

Public toilets, those in bistros, cafés or restaurants in France, generally don't have any. Unless I happen to forget, which is rare, I stuff my pockets and handbags with it.

In the camp, in a latrine if we managed to dig one, or in a remote corner, anywhere in the open, I first look for a tuft of grass, leaves, a stone, anything so as not to remain dirty and not to soil my clothes with excrement.

Hygiene has taken on new forms. It is indispensable for me in order to live with dignity.

I don't know how long I could have survived in *Block* 26 and what kind of work would have followed the sand-shovelling at the hangar. But, in spite of entire transportations that never enter the camp, in spite of almost daily selections, we are becoming too numerous at Birkenau. Above all, we have so many lice that the SS are afraid of catching typhus themselves. They are entitled to be vaccinated but they cannot be sure of being totally protected.

It is 5 December 1942, the worst hell of a day engraved in my memory. We are 6,000 at morning roll call, 1,500 at evening call. It is a Sunday, I think. Sundays are always the worst days of the week. The SS have time off and take the time to enjoy themselves. If it is not with their families, it is with us.

So, after a roll call lasting longer than usual, the *Kapos* lead us towards the electrified barbed wire at the entrance to the camp. We pack ourselves in between the high voltage and a small ditch which separates our strip of ground from the camp.

Our warders plant themselves in front of us. SS men and women. They hold their wolfhounds on leads. Endless waiting begins, with a plan well calculated by them, uncertain for us. We guess that they must be preparing a selection but we don't know their methods of selecting.

Generally, our executioners demand their victims be naked at the beginning of a selection. But it's a cold winter's day. Out of habit many comrades spontaneously start to undress. Others, sure of a fatal outcome, want to finish their lives themselves and move towards the electrified perimeter. From the height of the watchtowers volleys of submachine gun fire crackle and put an end to the rush of voluntary deaths.

Behind the barbed wire stand armed soldiers as well. We are truly encircled. We are hungry, we are thirsty, we are cold, we are afraid.

It never occurred to me to undress. I cannot accept this ultimate humiliation. Esther reacts like me. The majority do the same.

After a while that I measure in hours, our enemies change their formation and deploy themselves in a long corridor that winds up and down towards *Block* 25. The senior ranks stand on the left at the end of the corridor. The *Kommandant* is among them.

I can still hear our silence! Then abruptly the orders fall like whiplashes. Our group struggles forward towards the narrow corridor formed by the SS. Once we have jumped over the ditch, the game of obstacle-racing can begin. We run after life or death, no one knows. Esther runs just behind me. We notice that our executioners on the left are armed with bent canes, those on the right have whips and truncheons.

This selection soon proves to be a hundred times worse than all those we have experienced until now. With their hooked canes, the SS on the left catch their victims by the neck and have no difficulty in making them fall. Soon after the SS on the right make them stand up again with baton blows or whiplashes to chase them out of the line. A rearguard in uniform throws itself with bare hands onto those who are unable to get up, dragging them out of the race to form a barrier between the race for life and those eliminated from life by it.

The scenario has been worked out with clockwork precision. I see the comrade in front of me in the race fall down; I hear another body fall behind me. I know it's Esther. I keep on running. I don't turn to look. A feeling of loneliness overwhelms me. I am not going to die today. At the end of the corridor we fall on top of one another, out of breath. We get up, stupefied and silently count ourselves. Three-quarters of our workforce has disappeared in an unimaginable manner, as we will learn at roll call.

There is no time to draw breath. Immediately we have to line up to be counted and listen to the *Kommandant*'s speech. I remember his exact first words: 'Ihr seid zum Leben gewählt' (You have been chosen to live!). I don't remember anything else, though his speech was long. Because in the meantime our eyes are turned towards the entrance of the camp where our selected comrades remain. We see the trucks arrive, I count 17 of them. And the shuttle begins during the speech. We see our comrades climb up, every single one, all resisting. We hear them scream.

I still hear those screams in my nightmares. Their shrieks are louder than the words of the *Kommandant*. Besides, his words are irrelevant to us. We do not believe we are going to live. We are only reprieved.

But our comrades, whom we can hear screaming, know as well as we do that they are going to be gassed. They howl in the face of death. Have you ever heard human beings howling in the face of death?

According to the collaborator Darquier de Pellepoix, they

47

only gassed the lice. There were too many of them and we with them. We truly died with our lice in the gas chambers. We can swear to it because we know.

The camp administration, after this massive selection, is not satisfied with simply counting us. No one knows who died, who is alive. The Nazi bureaucracy needs to make a new register. The *Schreibstube* and *Politische Abteilung* commandos will have some work to do.

After this first roll call, therefore, we walk back to the *Block Sauna*. There we settle down on the ground as well as we can to wait for the next events. The *Schreiberinnen* with their old registers call us up, thousand after thousand. From zero to 1,000, 2,000, then 3,000 etc. As I do not have to answer until beyond 20,000, I observe that at the call of many thousands no one stands up to move forward to the registration tables. The dead with a number answer by their absence and their silence at the call of their thousand. Four thousand five hundred names have to be struck out of the register.

In between 20,000–30,000, there are only two of us who walk to the registration tables to let it be known that we still exist and again be registered to confirm it.

We leave the *Sauna* for another surprise. Fumigation of the entire camp is the order of the day. For a whole week we are going to be locked up in one *Block* and we will never know how or by whom the camp is going to be cleaned. Perhaps by newly arrived convoys or *Sonderkommandos* kept in reserve. It is difficult to imagine any confusion worse than ours.

At first we can spread ourselves throughout the whole available space. We have no more superiors, but we are still granted the morning unnameable infusion and the evening soup. Nothing else – we are not working.

There is no roll call either. During this time of rest we are devoured by hunger, thirst and lice. We live with our excrement. To start with we try to use only the corners of our

48

Block for bodily functions. But the number grows larger and larger of those who no longer have the strength to move. So we settle ourselves on the high levels and only get down to relieve ourselves on the ground floor. We need to be strong enough to drag ourselves to the door for the *herbata* or the soup. Many remain lying down and die, sometimes in their excrement down below. Those who die at the top are thrown down. There is nothing else to be done.

The 5 December registration can't have been very useful. We are no longer the same number of living when the door of our *Block* opens and we can at last leave the nauseating atmosphere we have been breathing for days and nights.

It is daytime and we feel some kind of intoxication at breathing the fresh air. Some comrades faint. But the *Aufseherinnen* SS are here to push us around and make us work.

While we were surviving in these modern-day Augean stables, the Birkenau camp has been cleaned, renovated.

Trains keep on arriving day after day, usually at night. New women detainees, who were 'lucky' enough to get into the camp and get a tattoo on their left forearms, are filling the *Blöcke* once again.

I think that it is from that time that they started to tattoo a small triangle under the numbers of the Jewish women deportees, to distinguish them still better from the Aryan women. Later on, after hundreds of thousands of tattoos, they started counting from the beginning again, prefixing the number with an 'A'.

The SS administration always tried to conceal the exact number of victims. Some 'revisionist' historians take advantage of this. History will render us justice: we were gassed in millions and the night sky of Auschwitz will blush red at it for ever.

Our first task is to make bundles of all our blankets and carry them, running, to be fumigated. The *Aufseherinnen* run alongside us setting the tempo with truncheon blows.

Then we return to the *Sauna* where a ceremony, almost the same as the initiation session on our arrival, awaits us: a cold shower with no means of drying ourselves, followed by a complete shave of our heads.

Meanwhile, unknown commandos empty our *Block* of our dead and our excrement, to return it to us as a dwelling place. In the evening we will once again find a *Koje* to sleep in and prepare ourselves for the endless roll calls, until death when we lose our strength through starvation or work.

I have memories of my last days at Birkenau which are fragmented but vivid. First of all, I feel quite alone. There is no one who needs me to raise their morale so my own is sinking.

Sleeping is practically impossible. In our *Koje* I am with strangers. We are so cramped that we spontaneously fit around one another like a jigsaw. It's the best way of keeping warm and we toss and turn with perfect timing.

For work, new commandos are formed each day. The point of our activity often escapes me. I empty watertight ditches. I am provided only with an empty tin tied to the end of a long stick to do it with. Sometimes unfortunate comrades slip down into the ditch. It is their death sentence. Anything will do to make fertiliser.

I have also dug inside the camp. To break into the frozen soil I need the full weight of my body. We are preparing, it seems, the ground for future gardeners.

Outside the camp I carry stones held tightly against me – to build roads, they say. The distance we have to carry them varies but the quantities are fixed. Carrying too many or for too long leads to death by exhaustion.

In this commando there are several deaths each day. We have to bring them back to the camp. We have been counted out in the morning; they must have the same number of workers when we return.

The evening when I carry the leg of a dead comrade who four of us have to bring back, I feel it will soon be my turn. It is a strange sensation to feel you are dying.

At evening roll call a *Läuferin* runs through the *Blöcke* to say that all biologists must present themselves at the gate of the camp the following morning. To survive or to die, that is my question. To be realistic, I am going to die or I am going to become a biologist. My taste for pathological anatomy could come in handy. I do have knowledge in this field and the practical experience I gained during the two years I spent in the Laboratory of Pathological Anatomy at the Paris Medical School is going, with a bit of luck, to save my life.

The next day after roll call I refuse to leave with the external commando. It is a risk to run, on account of the daily selections in which the victims are women who are totally exhausted and try to hide to get some rest, even for one day. They take refuge among the sick of the *Reviere* or camouflage themselves at the bottom of a *Koje*. The staff who stay behind are there to track them down.

After the departure of the commandos I walk towards the camp gate. Other detainees are there already. I am neither the first nor the last. To be chosen I will have to convince them.

To the first SS man who comes and asks me what I am doing there, I answer that I am a biologist. When it is my turn to enter the office of the SS officer, I tactically choose to tell the truth. It is my good fortune to be able to explain myself in German.

Without knowing for what purpose they are going to use biologists, I insist in my interrogation that I am advanced in my medical studies and that I chose to specialise in pathological anatomy. I state with aplomb (but it is also true) that I am well versed in preparing microtome slices, dyeing them and examining them in the microscope for diagnoses.

I know full well that my SS examiner is not interested in the preparation of samples of acute appendicitis or lung tissue ravaged with TB, not even in the examination of biopsies to determine whether a tumour is malignant or not.

By the end of this interview I have managed to be pre-selected as a biologist. I seem to correspond to a type of detainee no longer sought for her muscular strength but for her grey matter. I'm ordered to stay in the camp until further notice so I can be ready for transfer to another camp. That is already a first piece of luck, for in between the roll calls I still have to attend, I can rest inside my *Block*, escaping from work and the winter cold.

I will also eat better and eat hot food. In fact, I am at the *Block* in the afternoon when the *Stubovas* bring the *Kübels* of soup for the evening distribution. I soon realise why we only get a thin and tepid liquid in our bowls after work and roll call. The moment they arrive the *Blockova* asks for the big containers, supposedly thermostatic, for her to go fishing in with her ladle. She serves herself first, of course, followed by her acolytes, each to several helpings. For the first time, I see there are a few pieces of meat and fat, as well as vegetables other than swede or peelings. The soup is thick enough. The *Blockova* sees I'm looking and serves me to buy my complicity.

That is how these supervisors, who are corrupted by the SS, manage to live at the expense of their comrades. It is part of their way of organising to find assistant executioners, more or less conscious, among the deportees themselves.

There would have been no point in refusing this bowl of soup which will give me back some strength. But it revolts me at the same time. I understand during these few days that I cannot survive that way. I must live differently or else it is better to die.

I will not change into a wolf; I will remain a human being.

5 · Stabsgebaüde *Auschwitz*

It is nearly Christmas when the hour strikes for our transfer. At last! About ten of us gather at the gate of the camp. A lorry is waiting but we do know that we are not heading for the gas chambers and their chimneys which illuminate our nights.

At the end of this short journey, we stop in front of a grey, administrative-type building of several floors. It is the *Stabsgebaüde* of Auschwitz, the camp's headquarters.

We are still in the same concentration complex, in which right until the end, we will be just a cog, never knowing quite how vast it is or how many large and small camps are attached to it.

Our new camp is set up in the cellars of the *Stabsgebaüde*. The commandos which the HQ want to keep handy live underground.

Our new *Blockälteste* gives us a good welcome. Her name is Gerda and she wears a red triangle. She is German and has been an internee since 1933. It is the closest I have been to a communist since I left Germany myself that same year. She's a Berliner too. We will become friends. I do not know if Gerda is still alive. She certainly lives on in my heart. It is to men and women like her, German communists interned since the inception of the concentration camps in 1933 in Dachau, Oranienburg, Sachsenhausen, that many foreign deportees owe their survival. Throughout their long internment they were the first to organise the resistance in the camps and to help other nationalities to get actively involved. With great patience they succeeded in taking over power from the green or black triangles. The SS are well aware that they are dealing with enemies of the first degree. But thanks to them the SS have less trouble making their camps function properly and deep down they are lazy people dependent on bloody methods.

Gerda hands over all the new arrivals to Else – German, like her, but a black triangle, in charge of the cloakroom.

For the first time since I arrived at the camp in September we really have a hot shower. Then Else gives us clean clothes. Also for the first time I am entitled to the striped blue and grey outfit which will become a part of history. Lice are not allowed in here.

Gerda tells us we are in quarantine to verify our state of health. We will not be starting work straight away. It is a wonderful surprise.

After the hygiene session, we find sufficient food and rest in three-tier bunk beds, where there is a bed for each person. Our new comrades are at work but they welcome us with warmth when they return in the evening.

Before I speak of them, I owe a few lines to Else who saved my life. Here's how she did it.

After a few days there I notice that I am covered with lice again. One louse and you're dead: I know it only too well. Careful examination reveals that the hem of the striped dress I am so proud of is packed with lice eggs. There is no hope at all of getting rid of them on my own. I risk being sent back to Birkenau.

I decide to put my fate in Else's hands. She welcomes me into the cloakroom with kindness and changes my clothes from head to foot. It will remain a secret between the two of us. The result is a friendship to which I remain faithful.

The black triangle she wears means, in her case, prostitute. Else tells me her story, which is a very simple one. In Magdeburg she practised the profession some call the oldest in the world. It is at the time when young German women, the blonde, blue-eyed Aryans of the Hitler Youth, are prostituting themselves free of charge with carefully selected SS men to offer children to the Führer.

The professional prostitutes are closely watched by pimps of the Horst Wessel type, he whose sordid assassination will give Nazi Germany its national anthem. To manage to live Else simply charged more than the authorised rate. That was enough to send her to Auschwitz.

I will lose track of her when they open a brothel in the camp. Else tells me herself that she considers it a professional duty to take part in it. She doesn't want to leave the job of selecting the victims to the SS themselves. At the end of the day, in this brothel for detainees there will be professional women alongside volunteers who are ready to save their skins, even at that price. The choice by the SS of a few unwilling victims is reduced, thanks to this conscious awareness of their duty among professionals like Else.

Whenever I come across prostitutes in the streets of Paris, my heart skips a beat as I think of my friend. They are victims of our society. There will not be prostitutes for ever, as there will not be wars for ever, or unemployment. I have respect for Else of Auschwitz.

The third comrade, who throws herself into my arms by way of introduction, is Ella. She has all the bad marks against her: she is German, from Berlin, Jewish, a communist and a member of the resistance since Hitler's rise to power.

This dynamic, enthusiastic brunette with sparkling eyes has chosen a hard life. At fifteen she slams the door of her home behind her and breaks with her bourgeois family for good. Her political commitment makes her a refugee and she too ends up in France. A few years older than me, she has to work to survive. But at the same time she studies chemistry at the School and Museum of Arts and Crafts. She continues her political activity, together with her companion, who enrols in the International Brigades and dies alongside the Spanish Republicans.

For them, the anti-fascist war began on Spanish soil. Ella, arrested as a member of the resistance, arrived at Auschwitz without passing through Drancy, like many other Jews who were guilty of the knowledge that they must fight back.

She survived Auschwitz and remained in Germany, her homeland. But there was no longer one Germany: it was divided into two states. Ella chose her side to carry on the struggle. Ill, she found refuge in a voluntary death.

She was my first political guide. Ella is already working as a chemist in my new commando. We often have stormy discussions. Our main subject of discord is the German–Soviet Non-Aggression Pact, signed by Von Ribbentrop and Molotov. I don't understand; she explains. Others too will make this place of death, which is what a concentration camp is, into a school for life. Teaching one another is our intellectual form of resistance.

She introduces me to Annie, a Czech comrade from Prague. Annie doesn't know that she was the one to whom I was most attached but she kept my hexameter verses. A communist with clear and open views, she was expelled from her party after the Soviet intervention of 1968, when in the context of 'normalisation' more than a third of the communists who believed in the Prague Spring lost their cards.

I met Annie 30 years later in her beautiful city of Prague, during a tour organised for the New Year's Eve celebration at the end of 1975. Frankly, I only went so I could meet her. In her home she showed me a small book bound in red canvas, preserved like a relic, a future piece in a museum of the resistance, already exhibited many times. It was made by my own hands and contained the long poem in German I composed for her on her birthday in 1943.

This book was found by the SS during a search of our straw mattresses. Even if we are chosen for our grey matter, we are not protected against death, which continues to keep an eye on us.

56

Annie took it all upon herself without betraying the author. As I was Jewish, if she had turned me in, that would have been the end of my life. For her, *Volksdeutsche* and Aryan, it would have meant *Strafversetzung* (transfer to a punishment *Kommando*) to Birkenau. I still feel guilty about it. I wouldn't have been able to go on living if Annie had not got out of it.

A tree bears her name in the Avenue of the Righteous at Yad Vashem, near Jerusalem. I am not the only one who owes it to her that they came back.

Finally, there is Claudette, my future biology head of staff, a student of Marcel Prenant. She arrived at Birkenau in June 1942 as a volunteer, if I remember well, to join her husband. She bears on her forearm a number with four figures only. I do not know if any more longstanding deportees are still alive now as I write. I think it is she who explains to the new arrivals the work which awaits them after their period of quarantine.

6 • Taraxacum Kok-Saghiz

I still like dandelions. They saved my life as well. I respect these bright yellow flowers; I blow their winged seeds away so they will multiply; I eat their green, indented leaves in salad; and I remember the *kok-saghiz*, which belongs to the same Taraxacum family.

Its history goes back to the Russian Civil War and the foreign interventions the young Soviet Union has to confront after the victorious Revolution of October 1917. An economic consequence of the 'cordon sanitaire' with which the allies of capitalist Europe are attempting to strangle the newly born socialism is a shortage of raw materials, such as rubber, usually extracted from the hevea tree.

The Soviet scientists take part in the struggle against the effects of the imperialist war by embarking on some eager and in-depth research. They discover a variety of dandelion, the *Taraxacum kok-saghiz*, the root of which has about a seven per cent latex content which can be transformed into natural rubber. It is a useful discovery.

I don't know to what use the Soviet Union put this discovery. What is certain is that there were scientific publications on the subject and that there was a sizable stock of seeds.

When Hitler's armies tore into the Soviet Union on 21 June 1941, they made staggering progress – right up to the gates of Moscow and Leningrad.

The Nazis lack raw materials as well and to remedy the absence of natural rubber, their Bunawerke factory in Upper Silesia buys very cheap deportee labour from Auschwitz to manufacture artificial rubber.

But natural rubber is far superior. It is in Minsk that they will find the traitor who knows the *kok-saghiz* and who, in exchange for payment, collaborates in transforming the vast plains of Ukraine into a field of German natural rubber.

It is enough to put the good techniques which already exist into practice. The job of doing this is given to the *Kaiser Wilhelm Institut* in Berlin. To protect him from the revenge of his compatriots, the man from Minsk and his family are uprooted to Auschwitz.

As in the Krupp, Thyssen, AEG and I G Farben factories, the scientists of the *Institut*, high ranks in the SS, will purchase from their colleagues at Auschwitz those deportees whose grey matter or technical competence will save them from going to the front.

The man from Minsk, as a privileged civil worker, will be allocated the same task as us. He will not be with us; he will be against us.

Thus Claudette tells us that our boss owns one of the most important research institutes in Nazi Germany and that our commando *Pflanzenzucht* (plant cultivation) commando is supervised by learned intellectuals, officers of the SS.

The purchase of the necessary labour force for this research from the concentration camp is good business for both the *Kaiser Wilhelm Institut* and the *Kommandant* of Auschwitz.

Compared to a normal work force, we are cheap, and we increase the wealth of the SS who run all the camps dedicated to the Final Solution. But before that, we are exploited as slaves by the big German trusts, the *Konzerne*, i.e. the research institutes, which install their factories and laboratories around the perimeter of the camps.

They will not go short of hands or brains. They arrive every day, from all over Europe. They have total control over our working conditions; they fear neither strikes nor sick leave. Even our deaths mean nothing to them. We are immediately replaceable.

But we shall resist by surviving and sabotaging. Our SS are so primitive they believe we are loyal to save our lives. They do not even suspect that, for us, there are more important things than this life, which is so little our own.

Our commando consists of different sections. I shall belong to the 'laboratory' section which contains two scientific disciplines – biology and chemistry – and two artistic ones – drawing and photography. The other section, which makes us worthy of the name of *Pflanzenzucht* (plant cultivation), comprises agronomist–engineers and a multitude of women technicians responsible for cross-breeding, pollination, vegetable reproduction, experimental fields, greenhouses etc.

Finally, a third section, where the man from Minsk works too, is responsible for translation from Russian to German and experimental application of the contents of the works which the *Kaiser Wilhelm Institut* has helped itself to.

Our boss tailors his ambitions to match his budget for research and the upkeep of our grey matter. He decides to build a special camp for the female commandos, *Pflanzenzucht* and *Gärtnerei* (gardening) right next to the laboratory, greenhouses and experimental fields for *kok-saghiz*, but to make it financially viable by adding greenhouses for growing flowers and vegetables. This will be the main work of the second commando. The necessary male reinforcements will come from Auschwitz. We will, therefore, have many ways of securing vital contacts with the neighbouring camps.

This future camp will be called Raisko and will be open to welcome us in the spring. It will, of course, include the houses and villas of our learned SS, the detachment of our wardens including an *Aufseherin* and the usual slave-drivers with their dogs.

There was only one successful escape, that by two Soviet prisoners, one of whom was Vera, my first Russian teacher.

The numerous camps in Upper Silesia belonging to the Auschwitz complex were mainly built by the deportees themselves. But there were also civilian workers, generally acting as foremen.

It is, therefore, totally impossible that the German population – located nearby and able to see the chimneys of the crematoria belching out their smoke; watching, like we do, the sky turn red at night – impossible that this population did not know what was happening in the camps.

For me, they are all accomplices, at the very least, because of their indifference and tacit assent.

Sonia needs our help and protection. She arrived at Birkenau with her husband and her baby in her arms. As usual, she was immediately separated from her husband. She replied to the SS in charge of allocations that she was a chemist and her baby was snatched away from her. They need chemists, not babies. She fought tooth and nail against the enforced separation and was struck repeatedly with a cudgel, on her head and elsewhere. The blows to the skull provoked lesions, luckily reversible with time. These in turn triggered violent epileptic fits, which at first were frequent. The SS never knew about these fits. Our combined solidarity, each time she had one, always protected her from the eyes of the enemy.

Our quarantine will not last 40 days. In any case, no SS doctor ever comes to examine us. I think the SS are afraid of typhus and want to make sure none of the new recruits of commando *Pflanzensucht* has the disease which is carried by rats and lice.

What matters for us during this waiting period is the chance to rest and regain some strength from the camp food. Gerda ensures it is distributed fairly and doesn't take her own share in advance.

We are able to get to know our co-detainees, to speak, discuss, and rediscover our humanity and dignity.

There is hardly any roll call in our cellar. The *Kapos* of the various commandos which set out from the *Stabsgebäude* are responsible for checking the work force in and out.

The SS, who are faithful to their traditions to the point of absurdity, even fix up a decorated Christmas tree for us in our dormitory.

The many colours of the glass balls shine in my dreams. Memories of my love at Drancy give me strength; hope will no longer abandon me.

One day in January we finally go outside into the fresh air, to form up in rows of five and go to our posts.

The memory I retain of my first laboratory is one of temporary shacks. There are three biologists: Claudette, Mella, who passed herself off as a doctor but was not really one, as I will discover after liberation, and me. Ella and Sonia are chemists; Edith and Salla are translators and there is little Wanda who will draw pictures of our cuttings of *kok-saghiz*, following the instructions given by Claudette.

The rest of the commando, under the leadership of the tall Wanda, our *Kapo* and an agronomist, continues its walk towards the greenhouses and fields.

The SS officer on duty, a *Scharführer*, if I am not too lost among the grades of this criminal army, is an exception to the general rule of sadism which characterises our executioners. I mention him, because as the only exception to the rule, he is sent to the eastern front soon after.

I met Sonia in Paris on the twenty-fifth anniversary of the liberation of Auschwitz, commemorated at Salle Pleyel. She runs an important chemical factory in Kharkov. Together we went to the Paris café La Coupole, the rendez-vous we agreed upon at Raisko, to meet regularly on Saturday afternoons, should we escape from our programmed death. Sonia has had her tattooed number removed, and shows us a scar in its place. I am not to see her in 1985 when I take a cruise on the Volga. Death struck her down too soon for that. Most of our lives have been shortened by at least ten years.

At the end of January 1943, distressing news reaches us. A convoy of women members of the French Resistance has arrived at Birkenau instead of Ravensbrück, the usual destination for such convoys.

I have always regarded this as proof that the Nazis wanted to apply the Final Solution to their most tenacious enemies as well.

These women came into the camp holding their heads high, singing *La Marseillaise*. The news of this act of courage and resistance spreads like wildfire and galvanises our will-power.

This convoy left Romainville on 24 January; the names of Danielle Casanova and Marie-Claude Vaillant-Couturier are whispered from one woman to the next.

There are many women in this group who shed tears for a husband, a companion, shot dead at the Mont-Valérien. Such is the case of Hélène, the wife of Jacques Solomon and the daughter of the great scientist Paul Langevin. There are many others, less well known. Almost all are communists.

Thanks to this convoy, I learned that the Resistance has been able to create conditions in the camp which can save human lives.

Claudette succeeds in having Jacqueline join our commando. She is, perhaps, a teacher of natural sciences and will make a perfect assistant in botany. Jacqueline, who is in touch with her comrades via the international political organisation of the camp, knows well their skills and qualifications. We welcome two brilliant chemists: Marie-Elisa, top scholar at the Faculty of Paris, and Mimi, the best student of the Faculty of Nancy. Hélène joins the team of biologists. Others join the *Kommando Pflanzenzucht* as

63

technicians; a few women resign themselves to the *Kommando Gärtnerei*.

Raisko is better than Birkenau. But we cannot save everyone. Danielle Casanova will die in May and the SS will be powerless to do anything about the flowers which pile up in her honour.

Our Polish women are annoyed; the weight of the French Resistance increases at Raisko with the arrival of the convoy of the '31,000'.

The laboratory building is naturally ready before the rest of the Raisko camp. Consequently, we leave the *Stabsgebäude* every morning for work, as do all the external commandos, in rows of five, a *Kapo* at our head, surrounded by our SS guards and their dogs. They enjoy hearing us sing all the way there.

Hélène is the life and soul of our group. I walk in the centre. Sonia is in between us. When one of her epileptic fits begins along the way, we grab her firmly under the armpits and drag her along with us. Then we strike up a song, preferably one which puts our guards in a good mood. They like *La Madelon* and *Kalinka*. As we walk briskly along, they are a hundred miles from our thoughts. And we are lucky that Sonia doesn't bite her tongue and that her fit always stops before we arrive. When we move to Raisko it becomes easier to hide her when she has her fits.

I don't remember the exact date of the inauguration of the special camp. We leave the *Stabsgebäude* and the comrades from other commandos for good. But we take with us Gerda as the *Blockälteste* and Grete as our doctor.

There is of course a roll-call area where we line up in the morning and evening. But our *Aufseherin* counts our two commandos fairly quickly.

In our *Block* there are three-tier bedsteads with a bed each. I choose the top one. A fresh straw mattress, a clean blanket: it's going to be a good place to sleep. Yet most important are the showers, the sinks and the toilets. We will be able to keep clean. I can still picture the first shower we took on arrival. We are all naked, lined up under the shower-heads, staring at one another as if we had never met before. Such close contact between our bodies is an embarrassment for some, a wonderful experience for others. I spot the body of a young Polish woman, more beautiful than the statues of Phidias and Praxiteles which I admired in my childhood in the museums of Berlin and Paris.

There is truly nothing more beautiful than a living body. Such beauty must not, cannot perish. This body, just like the frosted trees, gives me courage and the certainty we will see the end of our slavery.

There are two refectories, in order to separate, in principle, our two commandos. There we find long wooden tables, benches and a few chairs. It is up to us to organise this space. Each of us is free to remain alone but no one wishes to do so. Groups based on affinities naturally form up.

The largest collective is that of the Polish women, with Wanda, the *Kapo*, at their head, assisted by her friend Janka. But not all of them rally to her side. Then there are the French women, with Marie-Elisa and Jacqueline in charge. Marie-Elisa comes to me to suggest that I join their collective. I am touched but I refuse. I am traumatised by the withdrawal of my naturalisation by Pétain and do not know where I stand in relation to France.

Furthermore, in 1943 I did not yet understand the need to regroup by nationality or language. And, as at the *Stabsgebäude* I have made friends, my small group, although French-speaking, is more international. There is Ella the German, Sonia the Russian, Edith the Slovak and I, who feel that I have no roots anywhere.

Forming such a collective or group has several consequences, the foremost of which is a fair distribution of all food, both that which is given out by the camp and that which we manage to 'organise' ourselves. It is a material consideration but crucial. The other consequences are more of an emotional, moral, religious and, of course, political order.

The formation of groups according to nationality makes internal relations easier. It also assists contacts with the national collectives in other camps, the commandos acting as intermediaries. This creates the chance of international agreements and common actions, including contact with the partisans, the Polish maquis, who are near to the camp.

It is through this channel that the convoy of which Danielle and Marie-Claude are part manages to contact the partisans who in turn transmit to London a list of names of the women Resistance members, forgotten at Birkenau as though lost in the mists of time.

After the victory of the Red Army at Stalingrad, a decisive turn in the anti-fascist war, the Hitlerites take the threat of reprisals from London seriously.

Auschwitz remains the place spacially designated for the Final Solution of the Jews. It is not, therefore, a suitable place for the French Resistance women of the Romainville convoy. So the SS at Auschwitz are ordered to redirect the remaining survivors of 24 January 1943 to Ravensbrück.

Those comrades who remain at Birkenau are put in quarantine. Those from Raisko, who have benefited from better living conditions, only join the other group just before their departure.

We are heavy-hearted but we rejoice about this transfer. We are sad to see these staunch, courageous comrades leave, and full of joy because at Ravensbrück they will stand more chance of survival.

One need only compare the percentage of survivors from the Jewish convoys with the others. At that time we did not know that these comrades who were leaving would later save our lives.

The sole aim of this glimpse into the future is to demonstrate just what can be achieved by exceptional efforts.

Raisko too is surrounded by barbed wire and we are under constant surveillance. And when now I am asked about the possibility of escape, the word 'impossible' springs to mind.

Yes, there were attempts. Those women generally ended up hanged on the roll-call area. I am thinking of Mala, the Belgian, who spat in the face of her executioner before she died.

We are on Polish soil, allegedly German. If you speak Polish or Russian you stand a slim chance of joining the maquis. Two Russian women, Valia and Vera, succeeded in escaping and I had to get a new Russian teacher.

But let's return to our lives at Raisko, which I am going to illustrate with anecdotes which explain how we managed to return from hell.

We nicknamed our new boss, the *Obersturmbannführer* (Major General of the SA) Joachim Cesar, 'Jules'. At the camp he will later marry a chemist named Ruth Weinberg. I could never rid myself of the thought that she was Jewish, but Hitler did say that it was up to him to decide. In any case, she arrived at Raisko with a testimonial indicating that she is *führungsfahig* (i.e. had leadership qualities). She is a chemist and will use our chemist comrades to prepare the thesis for her doctorate. I don't know why she chose the amount of Vitamin C in gladioli juice as her subject. Maybe she hoped to make up for the lack of oranges in the Third Reich with gladioli juice.

We are happy, anyway, to see beautiful flowers appearing in our laboratory. I don't recollect whether she was able to submit her thesis after the departure of the French chemists to Ravensbrück or not. But I am sure that gladioli juice has never been commercialised. We trusted Marie-Elisa, Mimi and the others to provide her only with sabotaged results. That was our form of resistance.

I had a letter from Ruth Cesar after liberation. She tells of her troubles during her flight from the Red Army and of the death of her baby. She cannot have been unaware that there were no children in Auschwitz, that they were all gassed, like those at Izieu, and that newborn babies were murdered in the camp.

Curiously, this letter reached me via the JOINT organisation. Her husband 'Jules' is on trial somewhere in Germany. The CIA is already seeking new anti-communist auxiliaries. Ruth wants me to have pity on her and be a witness in her husband's defence. She claims he always behaved humanely.

Humanely! I remember Germaine standing up all day in a field of onions. She was caught 'organising' some bulbs to bring back as a vitamin supplement to the food of her collective. In the evening, by the will of 'Jules' she will leave Raisko for Birkenau *strafversetzt*, a transfer which means she will effectively be punished by death for the small offence of theft. Yet Germaine survived, thanks to the departure of the French women to Ravensbrück.

A similar misadventure almost happened later on to Rosette who one evening was missing at roll call and was narrowly saved by the intervention of Stefanka, our new doctor. A *Strafversetzung* would have been fatal for her, a fragile Jewish girl scarcely out of adolescence.

No, not one of our SS in Raisko is human, otherwise they would have been sent to die on the eastern front as punishment. It is a risk none of them wants to run.

All the SS are criminals, men and women alike, including the *Waffen-SS*, from the heads of industry down to the concentration camp guards, by way of the intellectuals, scientists and artists.

I never went to Cesar's trial. I am not prepared to defend criminals.

Among our SS scientists, the ones specifically responsible for the laboratory, is *Sturmbannführer* Böhm. His springy, silent footsteps force us to be constantly on our guard. He is continually on our backs, trying to control everything and insisting that it is our duty to cooperate honestly and to attain full production capacity. He pushes this perverse logic to its extreme by explaining to us that if he were a prisoner of the Soviets, he would act in the same way.

On the eve of the evacuation of the camp, when we remind him of his words and promise to save him if he keeps us at Raisko until liberation by the Red Army, this coward lets us take our place in the death march.

The intelligent ones among the SS are worse than beasts. Until the very end they plan our deaths so that no witnesses will remain against them.

Hélène not only knows how to keep us going with songs, she also knows how to draw and is an expert on French wines. With our eyes seemingly riveted to our microscopes in order to draw dyed cuttings of *kok-saghiz* roots of all varieties, we have other drawing sheets in the half-open drawers of our work-tables on which she draws me a plan of my future studio and arranges the furniture in it in a practical manner. I was unable to save any of these plans but we dreamed together and I still long for a studio.

As for her knowledge of wines, when we take turns to cook imaginary meals, in an attempt to assuage our hunger, it is Hélène who pours the most appropriate wine to accompany each dish. After my return I never again drank red or white *vin ordinaire*. I benefited from these lessons too.

Our small camp has its own kitchens and, under the vigilant eye of Gerda, distribution is carried out fairly.

One day I walk past as potatoes are being delivered. I 'organise' some with the intention of sharing them among my small collective. A few yards further on, remorse takes hold of me. On reflection, I feel I've just robbed my own comrades instead of fighting the SS's will to exterminate us. I turn back and relieve both my conscience and my pockets of these few potatoes.

That day remains for me, no doubt for me alone, a memorable one. I have just taken a big step forward in my consciousness and I proudly proclaim it to my comrades. I will no longer rob us, for it is contrary to the spirit of solidarity; I will 'organise' for it is consistent with the spirit of resistance.

So, what can we 'organise' around our camp? Obviously everything the SS management refuses to give us and which we need in the way of food, medicine or cultural material.

I must repeat that every deportee who 'organises' knows that, if discovered, he or she is likely to die. But death is so omnipresent that we no longer fear it.

Through the activities of the *Gärtnerei* commando we have access to vegetables such as tomatoes, carrots and onions, to name but a few essential ones. We 'organise' them for our own needs, but also for use as barter. There are two methods of transporting them. For ourselves, we generally hide these products in the hollows of our bodies which are accentuated by our thinness: between the breasts, under the arms, around the legs; or we put them in our knickers which we have carefully equipped with elastic. For barter, which requires a certain quantity of a product, we use the baskets in which the *koksaghiz* plants are usually carried, and we rely for solidarity and for their need to exchange things on the external commandos coming from Birkenau, and especially from Auschwitz.

Among these are Frenchmen from the convoy of the '45,000' – reliable men like Eugène. But there are also German political prisoners like Otto, who becomes my lover.

To avoid being caught, we must 'organise' the vegetables the day before they are needed. Early in the morning, when the commandos from Auschwitz are just arriving, I leave the laboratory with a basket on my arm. It contains, for example, tomatoes covered with a good quantity of *kok-saghiz* which I have to take to the greenhouses. Otto waits for me at the entrance, to take charge of the basket. Most of the time the tomatoes are hidden in the soil on the floor of the greenhouses and they won't be handed over to the men until the evening when they return.

'Hole-head', one of our SS men, with a skull cracked at the eastern front, is a great expert at searches. While carrying out his systematic work he turns over the soil and comes across our tomatoes. This makes him furious, as he hasn't caught the culprit red-handed. So he says nothing, removes the tomatoes, and everything has to be done all over again.

I often volunteer, as does Otto, to be on duty on Sundays in the greenhouses. We slip under the plant-tables and make love in the semi-darkness and humid heat. We also dispatch green or flowering plants to be used as gifts for the internal senior staff of the camp to make sure they close their eyes and mouths. In this way, our infirmary is enriched by a few useful medicines, requested by our doctor comrade Stefanka. We manage to rid ourselves of Grete, who is too frightened and inclined to confide in the SS.

Personally, I managed to enrich myself with three books in German, my cultural treasure, but I was unable to keep them right to the end. They are Goethe's *Faust*, *Ulenspiegel* by Charles de Coster and an anthology of Heine's poems. *Ulenspiegel*, with its mockery of the Spanish occupying force, does most to buck up my courage.

Some of the French women from the convoy of the '31,000' managed to adapt the text of Molière's *Le malade imaginaire*. Thanks to them, in 1943 I experienced my most wonderful New Year's Day at the Raisko camp.

Prepared in great secrecy, shared by all except our SS, all who are not members of the cast make up an audience which is filled with admiration for an exceptional performance of the *Malade*, one which in my memory surpasses those of the Comédie Française. These performers, however, are all inexperienced amateurs, and all women.

But what matters is the laughter, the laughter of the audience, the laughter on the improvised stage, laughter long forgotten, human laughter, the laughter which signals our victory.

About a year after my arrival at Birkenau I have a premonition in the form of a dream. My doctor friends from Drancy are about to arrive. Our contacts within the *Schreibstube* confirm my dream. I try immediately to save Denise. It so happens that we have to accompany a lorry-load of our dirty laundry to Birkenau. While it's being unloaded we run towards the newly arrived women's *Block*. I learn that Denise has a sister, Françoise. When my intervention bears fruit, it is Françoise who comes, alone, to Raisko as our second draughtswoman. Death has already beaten Denise: it strikes fast.

It is during our expeditions to Birkenau that we discover that the gas chambers do not have the capacity to deal with all the convoys. I saw with my own eyes rectangular ditches, full of quicklime, the smell of which chokes us. On the edge, a doll, a toy lorry. And Annie tells us that the day before they threw in the weakest ones, still alive.

I see my first love once more. He arrived in the same convoy and was brought into Auschwitz. Having rid itself of the Jews from all over Europe who had become refugees in France, Vichy is now getting rid of its own Jews. Our love, which may have been only on my side but which helped me to live for a year, is dead. We cannot find the words to bring us close together, words for the future. In 1944 Sam is part of a convoy to Buchenwald. After my return I learn that he died there shortly before the deportees of that camp liberated themselves by force of arms.

I also lost Otto in 1944. A German communist, interned since 1933, he arrived at Auschwitz from Lublin (Maidanek). He knows the Red Army is getting closer each day, as is victory. But how to get out of a camp like Auschwitz?

I don't know whether he chose the right method or not. The German political prisoners are divided on the question when the SS camp management, getting wind of defeat, proposes to enrol them in the defence of the fatherland, in the uniform of the *Wehrmacht*. Otto accepts in the hope of joining the partisans and the Red Army. I never heard from him again.

In the same way we go to Birkenau for our laundry, we go to Auschwitz, to the men's camp, for our teeth. Our gums are receding dangerously and bleeding; our teeth are very loose.

Dental care at Auschwitz is in the hands of the Polish men. In return for the work they do on our teeth in a well-equipped surgery and the heat treatment they carry out on our gums, they demand that we masturbate them at the same time. We cannot refuse without running the risk of being badly treated. Then, each one having completed her duty, in the waiting room we receive a packet of margarine, thrown over the partition door by an anonymous hand, and we share it between us.

These expeditions allow me to get to know other German political prisoners, like Ludwig, Ernst, Papy, who do not share Otto's view and do not want, under any circumstances, to run the risk of dying wearing a German uniform. As they occupy positions of responsibility inside the camp, I believe they managed to escape in the last months. I remember a foreshadow of international fraternity which occurred on 21 January 1944. An invitation to gather in Gerda's room for a nocturnal vigil is whispered from woman to woman. It's the anniversary of Lenin's death. The room is tiny; Gerda could invite no more than a few of us. All nationalities are

73

represented. I am proud to be part of this commemoration, a symbol of unity and hope, a promise of loyalty.

The SS had wind something was happening that night. The women who know about it keep quiet. The others utter vague remarks about it. Gerda is interrogated and threatened with *Strafversetzung*. She remains silent. She will return alone to Birkenau.

It was after this brief ceremony, when each person present gave, in a few words, her reasons for believing in the inevitable defeat of fascism and the no less certain coming of socialism as a superior form of society, that I decided to join the Communist Party.

After the Jews, the most numerous group in the camp are the Polish women. At Raisko I met Magda, who calls herself a socialist, and Wanda – not the *Kapo* but our photographer – who is a communist and lives with our *Blockälteste* Gerda, far from the rest of her compatriots.

Both these women are close to us. Together they promised us that if they survived, they would make a film based on our mutual recollections. This film is called *La dernière étape* (the final stage) and, from our point of view, there has never been a more faithful testimony or a better kept promise. In this film I found myself back in the place of the young girl separated from her mother at the entrance to the camp.

As for the other Polish women, they are nationalists, Catholics and anti-Semites. As there are priests among the detainees in Auschwitz, our Polish women receive consecrated bread from time to time and can therefore take communion. Even after they have celebrated Easter, their anti-Semitism remains just as visceral.

Before our French compatriots from the convoy of the '31,000' leave for Ravensbrück, other Jewish resistance members, less French for being immigrants or born of immigrants, arrived to reinforce mainly the *Gärtnerei* commando. There are also other French-speaking comrades, such as Belgians, and a few Dutch women.

I recall a Romanian and two Hungarians, very withdrawn, terrorised, with death in their eyes. They know hundreds of thousands of their people have been annihilated on arrival at the camp. We also see Czechs, Slovaks, Greeks and Yugoslavs arriving.

This international influx will modify our internal structures after the departure of the '31,000'.

Most of the collectives have restructured. Claudette, with whom Françoise remains, welcomes Mella and Sonia. Ella joins a group of young Czechs who need political instruction. With a new conscience I leave the dining room of commando *Pflanzenzucht* and join the multinational French-speaking collective of commando *Gärtnerei*. They are all Jewish and most are communists. Guiza, a Belgian comrade, probably the highest-ranking at the party level, takes charge of our organisation.

My political convictions have evolved considerably in the camp. I have accepted the German–Soviet non-aggression pact, having understood that the non-intervention in Spain led to the failure of the Popular Front and facilitated, via Munich, the criminal alliance of the Vichy French fascists with Hitler.

My own experience of the accession of Hitler in Germany in 1933 has already taught me that it is the disunity of the left forces, who still comprise the large majority, which is to blame. It permitted an army of crime, financed by the great Ruhr industrialists in order to bring to heel the German working class and its four million unemployed, to seize power by apparently democratic means.

As for Pétain, ex-ambassador to Franco's Spain, he was also the placeman of the French capitalists who preferred Hitler to the Popular Front, occupations of their factories and paid holidays for the workers.

I will never forget that evening in autumn 1944 when I asked to be admitted to the underground Communist Party of Raisko. In front of a panel of cadres, I give an account of my life and my political background. With my two women mentors I pace up and down the corridor, awaiting the end of the deliberations. When the door of the refectory opens, the answer is 'yes'.

Today I still believe that if it had not been for Hitler, exile, war and deportation, I would have retained the idealistic position of German social democracy, just like my parents. I still want socialism, as they did. I remain faithful to their ideals, but I have changed parties.

At Birkenau, Auschwitz, Raisko and the camps that followed, my childhood dreams of freedom, social justice and human rights lost their utopian character and became objectives for active revolutionary struggle.

I left behind for ever the salons where the world is changed with words; I placed myself on the side of the oppressed, the exploited. It is a decisive choice.

News travels well at Auschwitz and its annexes. It comes from contacts with the nearby Polish maquis, from newspapers and conversations overheard between the SS, and finally, from crystal radios built by detainees at great risk to their lives.

But our best guide is the sight of the SS's faces growing longer by the day. They cannot hide from us the victory at Stalingrad, or the Provence and Normandy landings, or the unstoppable advance of the Red Army.

We are very worried about our future, living close to the gas chambers and the crematory ovens which are in operation day and night.

We gain pleasure from hearing the dull sound of friendly guns, from being awakened at night by air-raid warnings. Our victory approaches. But will we live to see it? Many comrades believe that the SS will not leave any trace of their crimes and evil-doings behind them and that they will blow everything up at the last minute.

Not everyone shares that view. We have seen comrades arriving from Polish camps which have already been evacuated. We are also being used as a cover. The SS are sure the Soviet Union will not bomb the concentration camps. We have therefore opened negotiations with our torturers.

Perhaps some of these negotiations were successful as when the Red Army arrived to liberate Auschwitz the camp was not empty. Later on I learned that the liberators arrived on 27 January 1945, the day after my twenty-seventh birthday.

But for us the most terrible period of all begins on 18 January with the evacuation of the Silesian camps. We still face more than three months between life and death in the worst conditions.

7 • Death March

Jules, Ruth, Böhm, Hole-head and the others don't trust us when we guarantee their safety if they lead us to our liberators. They are scared out of their wits, because the soldiers we are waiting for know all about their crimes. These cowards will take flight and disappear out of sight.

We are left in the hands of the lower-ranking SS, who still execute orders given by the last Auschwitz *Kommandant*, for whom our lives are completely worthless. We gather up what is left of the food and our treasures. Mine are the books I want to save.

After a final roll call to empty all imaginable hiding places, our column starts moving slowly, in rows of five, to join a huge procession which has, for us, no beginning and no end, and moves towards an unknown destination. This regrouping by commando is good because we are surrounded by comrades and friends.

The SS who escort us, men and women with dogs, have put their luggage in a cart which we have to push and pull in turn.

We don't walk fast; nobody has ordered us to dawdle but we would have liked the Soviet vanguard to catch up with us.

Rosette's feet are terribly painful and she is unable to follow us. We lift her up onto the cart, which becomes even heavier, but a human life depends upon it.

We walk for days and nights in search of a ghost train. We try to sleep, flopped on top of one another on a concrete floor, with only our body warmth to protect us. We also find shelter in a cellar full of coal. Fortunately, it is too cold for the lice.

Snow is falling; the ground is frozen; we have nothing to eat or drink; we are dirty again, exhausted. We throw away anything that will lighten our march. I throw away my books. During our march we have not met anyone except death. In my memories of it everything is dark, in spite of the snow. Comrades too worn out to go on drop out of line and slip to the ground or try to flee. It is impossible to hold them back or lift them up again, even with several of us helping. And it would be fatal for us to stop. We hear the crackling of sub-machine guns at irregular intervals. Their noise accompanies us. We have no doubt as to its significance. The only ones we leave behind are our dead.

During that march I experienced the most atrocious thirst. I throw myself onto the snow which is piling up on the ground. I eat it in handfuls, unable to stop. My comrades are alarmed and fear for my sanity. So, in pairs, they grab me under the armpits and force me to walk in between them. They prevent me from bending down and gathering more and more of this dirty snow.

Then we find a train. It has no carriages, only open-air platforms. We pile ourselves on them, more than a hundred on each one, and our journey continues, under a leaden sky.

We are all standing; resting is out of the question. But we get ourselves organised. Half of us stay standing up, packed tightly against one another. This leaves more room for the other half who sit down and manage to sleep like this, so great is their fatigue. Secretly, I continue to eat the snow from the edges of the wagon. From time to time, taking my turn to squat down, I doze off a little.

I know neither the date nor the day of our arrival at Ravensbrück, nor how long we stayed there.

But I do know that the three months of wandering which still lay between us and our liberation were to be the worst time in the entire duration of my deportation. Until the very end, we will not know whether it is life or death which awaits us at the end of the road.

8 • Ravensbrück

We stayed at Ravensbrück for a few weeks, in a tent, probably in the vicinity of the lake. I only discovered this 40 years later when I was part of a delegation of ex-deportees who were guests of the Committee of Anti-Fascist Members of the Resistance in the German Democratic Republic.

The influx of survivors of the death march has not been taken into account in the organisation of the camp, and certainly not in the kitchens. We only continue to survive thanks to the solidarity of comrades from the French convoy of the '31,000', who arrived here a few months before us.

They come surreptitiously in the night and bring us whatever they have saved from their own rations of soup and bread.

On our side, the sharing is done rigorously. At Rose's instigation, a single spoon is used as a measure for all of us and we take turns to have a spoonful of soup until it is all finished.

We operate in this way often, especially when, following the occasional distribution of a liquid pompously called coffee, we find at the bottom of the *Kübel* a kind of thinly chopped straw which fills our stomachs and settles our diarrhoea.

Sleeping in that tent poses a serious problem. There are, it's true, three-tier bunk beds made of a few planks. There are no straw mattresses but what matters are the planks. We manage to find a place at the bottom, thinking we will have the advantage of greater mobility. We are four to this bed: Rosa, Ania, Rosette and I. Ania is tall and Rosette small: they stretch themselves diagonally. The other diagonal is for Rose and me.

We have not thought of everything, though. The snow is

melting and water seeps into our tent. It stagnates a few cen-
timetres from our planks. At the start we have seven planks.
Three of them will be stolen – snatched or conned out of us –
leaving four of us on four planks, scarcely protected from the
water, which we can reach with our hands.

It is crucial to keep hold of the remaining planks and we
organise a rota for guard duty. At least two of us stay on the
bed at any one time while one or two of the others tries to
bring some life back into their legs by splashing around in the
icy water.

We are not allowed to leave the tent. We are freezing and
even tightly huddled together in our group of four on our
four planks, we can't keep warm.

Our comrades have invented a new form of solidarity. They
come at night to fetch one or other of us and warm us up in
between their bodies under their blankets. In this way I get to
meet Louisa, who did not get to Ravensbrück via Raisko but
via quarantine instead. During the daytime I am unable to
recognise her.

For me, Ravensbrück is a long succession of nights without
days. So we are fairly pleased to be leaving this transit camp
for a new destination. I think there are about a thousand of us
leaving, in accordance with the usual practice of Nazi
convoys. In no time the train carries us further north.

9 • Malchow

Our new camp is still under the administration of Ravensbrück. I was only able to locate Malchow in Mecklenburg province much later on when I was able to consult an atlas.

It is a small camp planned to hold 2,000 detainees. There will be 3,000 mouths to feed including ours. We are not made welcome.

I don't know what the commandos which leave this camp really do. In my camping youth, the Mecklenburg, with its numerous lakes and the Baltic Sea a little further on, was always a holiday region. I cannot imagine an industrial zone there. It is the land of the *Junkers*, big land-owners who exploit the peasants for agriculture and cattle-rearing. Hitler recruited from there country squires with double-barrelled names and promoted them to the ranks of the SS. They have easy access to our extremely cheap labour force.

In fact, from this camp we are bought to work on the land. Each day the call resounds for volunteers to work outside. My collective nominates me as I speak German.

That is how I came to spend my days at Malchow among a family of small peasants. They too know where we came from, who we are. There is no conversation between us.

I turn over the earth, plant, hoe, bending all day long over the soil, which seems so far away from me. As a reward, I receive a good country soup around midday; it is very thick and I eat it alone at a table in the house. My stomach being satisfied, I can leave my camp soup to be shared among my comrades.

I think it is at Malchow that I celebrate, for the first time,

International Women's Day, on 8 March. We have 'organised' what we need for a good round tart. We grate raw potatoes and mix them with grated carrots. The top is decorated with the green part of a leek. I cannot recollect our speeches but the tart was good. I bequeath you the recipe. We feasted on it while singing the *Internationale* in very low voices.

We also got to know each other better in our little group, each one telling a bit of her life story to the others.

One of us is a diamond cutter. After her story I dream all night of a cascade of multi-coloured gems.

At Malchow we feel the end of the Great Reich is near. Those of us who go to the market town see cars full of refugees from the east. They are fleeing from the Red Army, who have already recaptured territories lost in 1917 and those stolen by Poland a long time ago. Their panic spreads through the population which lets itself be dragged into exile. It's their turn now.

There's no more work around to make the SS a profit. So we are on the move again, in convoy to our final camp.

At Magdeburg our train is bombed. From our wagons we see our slave-drivers run to take cover. Some of our SS throw themselves under our wagons. We remain stoic, locked in under a deluge of fire. After the alarm, the train leaves with us and them. It stops in Leipzig, a big city. Our new camp comes under the administration of Buchenwald.

10 · Leipzig

As for this final camp, we will not even know where it is situated, whether it is in the centre of town or outside it, or what kind of work is demanded of the ordinary detainees. We will only know our own *Block* with its bunk beds, where we lay almost all day long, totally exhausted.

Wherever we arrive now, there are too many of us and we are not expected for work or for food. Luckily, from time to time, an *Aufseherin* comes and asks around for volunteers to bring in and stack the vegetables for the soup. We move quickly and efficiently. 'Organising' is quite easy. We are so thin that hiding vegetables in the emaciated holes around our bodies and walking away with a large quantity of potatoes in our knickers poses no problem to us at all. This is how we survive.

There are 16 of us remaining in our collective of French speakers. Guiza and Rose oversee the fair distribution of food. I have never eaten so many raw potatoes. And I have never since wanted to eat any more, not even to remember how they tasted. The soup they bring us is just water with a few pieces of swede and potato peelings swimming in it. We fish out the thick pieces of peeling for the weakest and the sick among us.

Don't imagine that even when we were lying down we were inactive.

Rose, who knows how to sew, invents a pattern for slippers, easy to cut and to make out of the old blankets we have managed to get hold of. Under her supervision, our collective becomes a sewing workshop. These slippers will be used as barter to improve our food and are in great demand.

But our imagination runs wild when we hear the guns to the east and west of the camp. The two allied fronts are getting nearer each day. We are caught in between the two, as between pincers. How are we going to get out?

We are still wearing the striped clothes which make us easily identifiable. We must get civilian clothes. Nothing seems impossible to us. Rose, who is certainly not lacking in imagination, requisitions all our decent blankets and we start making dresses, skirts, jackets – all tailored to fit, an outfit for each of us.

We put on these civilian clothes as soon as they are ready, wearing our striped dresses on top. We hardly look any fatter and we are just as warm with our double clothing as if we were covered with a blanket.

We can also feel the gentle warmth of an early spring. Our hearts are filled with hope. There are no gas chambers at Leipzig. In our mad calculations we think the Allies are racing one another to liberate us. Some bet on the Americans, others on the Russians. We listen to the guns. But we know we also have to reckon with the SS, who are still present and unpredictable. Our civilian clothes should help us to escape at the last moment.

On 13 April the Leipzig camp is evacuated. In rows of five we take to the road again.

11 • *The Final March*

We have no compass and we know which direction we are going in thanks only to the sun and the stars. We are heading east at a speed which must be in the order of one kilometre per hour. We drag ourselves miserably along.

We encounter many civilians as we pass through towns and villages. They dare not look at us. It is we who approach them, begging for peelings. They give us nothing, apart from one woman who slipped me a crust of stale bread. We feel they are dead scared, perhaps because of the SS. They also know that the end is near. As we pass through, we search the bins ourselves.

On the way we meet prisoners of war, walking in the opposite direction. Full of pity, they pass us four blankets. That will make two between eight of us. At nightfall we stop wherever we can and each group of eight spreads a blanket on the ground. We lay down in a circle, feet in the centre. The last one down pulls the second blanket over us. Our heads are on the outside, our bodies intertwined in the foetal position.

I remember the only occasion on which pieces of raw meat are distributed. We try to make a fire by knocking flints together but we have lost the skill of our cave ancestors. We eat the meat raw; we would have eaten anything. Don't foreigners call the French frog-eaters?

Later on, we come across streams of fugitives heading west and men armed with knives, bending over dead horses.

As on the preceding march, many comrades die during the ten days we spend on the road between the two fronts which are going to meet at the River Elbe. The SS still have orders to shoot anyone who is incapable of following the column or tries to escape. At night they surround us and keep watch. In spite of the risk of death, escapes increase. If you have to die it is better to liberate yourself than to fall on the ground, exhausted, to be shot at.

Ever since the beginning of the march, we have had a problem with Rosette. An adolescent, deprived of calcium, her feet hurt tremendously in their bad shoes and she can no longer put one foot in front of the other. We decide collectively that she should take the risk of escaping. She herself chooses the moment she thinks best to run away. With her small size, we rate her chances at the maximum.

A short distance from the village where she disappeared, our column collapses. We are seated or stretched out haphazardly. Suddenly we see Rosette coming back towards us, anxiously scrutinising our ranks. She is escorted by a young boy, about twelve years old, no taller than her.

I see the smile return to Rosette's face when she spots us. The story of her failure can be told in a few sentences. She had truly left us, in her civilian clothes, in the village, hoping to arouse pity among the villagers in order to find shelter and something to eat while waiting for the liberation army. When she took refuge under a porch, she came across the young boy who had been watching the column and saw where she came from. He threatened to denounce her if she didn't rejoin our painful procession. She resigned herself to it with the faint hope of finding us. Suspicious, the child stuck to her like a leech during her search. Yes, even children are our enemies. But luck was on Rosette's side.

We decide together that from then on there will not be any other escape attempts. It is better to stay together and stick it out to the limits of our endurance.

We abandoned our striped clothing a long time ago one night as we passed through a forest.

This zigzag march will last ten days, ten days of thirst and hunger beneath the bombings from both fronts.

At times we pass through woods where, out of fear, the SS delay our advance and make us lay down on the ground. We enjoy these moments of rest during which more and more comrades take off to the woods. The terrified SS have now given up chasing us. But they don't let us get away and they carry on killing those of us who fall down.

When we walk alongside fields it is up to whoever has the courage to throw herself into the field to collect some forgotten potatoes or pull out handfuls of rape-seed. We are well acquainted with the taste of raw potatoes; the cabbage-like taste of the rape leaves we chew is deliciously new and quenches our thirst a little.

The SS shoot the comrades who linger in the fields like rabbits. One must be quick and not venture too far. I nearly got caught but, as many of us run at the same time in search of something to eat, our guards don't have time to aim fire.

At the final night's halt our SS surround us as usual, in order not to lose us but also to save themselves from going to the front to be massacred. There is an abandoned windmill. We take shelter in it with the intention of not leaving the next day.

We do not yet directly know the extent of the fanaticism of the Hitler Youth, even in the last hours of combat. The following day three or four youths, only just 14 or 15 years old, armed with guns, dislodge us and force us to take to the road again. We will not go much further.

We reach the banks of the Elbe. Even today I do not understand what compels our SS towards the east, in the opposite direction to the increasing flow of German refugees. They are indifferent towards us and we expect nothing from them.

I see a bridge. It is intact but our executioners make us cross by ferry. We collapse on the bank completely exhausted.

'By the rivers of Babylon we sat down and wept...' waiting for death.

Hours go by and night starts to fall. I have a last shock. The SS are still there, unfortunately! We must get out of this place. I just about manage to arouse my comrades for a final effort; we lean up against the walls of the nearby houses. We won't escape from the view of our enemies who let us get on with it.

With the night come the bombers. After all this are we going to die under friendly fire? I advise my comrades to seek refuge inside the houses. We are in civilian clothing and it is best not to talk; all cats look black in the dark.

A few other comrades and I have slipped into a house and are packed inside. In the total blackout we can make out only vague silhouettes. Bombs are falling close by.

In the comings and goings of the night one sentence spoken in German changes our lives: 'The Ivans are here'. An empty space opens up around us as people move away.

When the sun rises, which it does emphatically on 23 April 1945, we leave that house, alive. On the spot where we had collapsed the day before, there is huge hole. The bridge has been destroyed.

The first sight I register for posterity in my amazement is a superb-looking Ivan, a Soviet soldier, perched on an abandoned baker's cart, his legs stretched apart, who in a gesture of triumph throws us the first loaf of freedom.

12 • The Taste of Freedom

Rosette has reminded me that we were liberated at Lauren-kirchen. Of course, we are not planning to stay and rot there. Death can still strike; the war is not over. Our direction is well-signposted – towards the rising sun.

The day before, we could hardly drag ourselves along; now freedom gives us wings. We advance laughing, singing and dancing. And Sarah points out a cherry tree in blossom. It really is spring time.

We walk alone along this road. An unusual sight and one which makes a military lorry driving in the same direction pull up alongside us. Red Army soldiers jump off; officers or ordinary soldiers, we don't know the difference.

None of us speaks Russian but some of us, who are of Polish origin, try to explain who we are by showing the tattooed numbers on our arms and pronouncing the dreaded name of Auschwitz. Thus, the opposite effect to the Tower of Babel is achieved. We rediscover a common language, Yiddish.

The soldiers pull photos out of their pockets, yellowed and dog-eared. They are of their families, their homes. They know what we are talking about; they have suffered like we have. That is why they are among the first to the front. To smash Hitlerite fascism is to avenge their own dead.

Victorious yesterday, by meeting up with the American army on the Elbe, today they are pulling back from the front.

They lower the back of their lorry and help us climb into it. We sit in the middle of them. They hide us under a ground sheet.

What they are doing is no doubt prohibited by army regulations. But we belong to the same community of 'judeo-bolsheviks', according to Hitler's definition. What they are doing is in keeping with the family spirit of the Jewish diaspora.

They take us with them so that we can truly become survivors who will give evidence on their behalf as well as on our own.

We reach the village where their quarters are. Their first concern is to find lodgings for us. They requisition a farm. The owners will have to go and live somewhere else! Yet they will be responsible for our food supply. And our new friends will ensure that this is the case for the whole of our stay in this village.

I know we must avoid overeating. Our bodies are no longer used to normal feeding. Many comrades died after their liberation because they were too eager to appease their insatiable hunger.

On our farm there are hens and rabbits. We ate them despite my advice, and everyone got diarrhoea, including me.

I remember a day when, in the presence of our farmers and against their will, our lieutenant asked us what we had eaten. He didn't like what he heard. He pulled out his gun and placed it on the table, demanding meat for us. Our farmers went to the bottom of their vegetable garden and started digging. They had a well-stocked cache and we never lacked for anything after that.

Our protectors also helped us to dress correctly by opening all the owners' wardrobes for us. We only took what we needed. I also took a watch.

Together we celebrate May Day. On that day it is the Red Army which brings our food, but it is we who do the cooking. What the dishes or the drinks were has escaped my memory. But I remember the toasts. Each man and woman lifted their glasses to the definitive defeat of fascism, to victory and peace for ever, to freedom and happiness for all, to socialism in a fraternal world.

Love is also in the air. Both we and they are in need of it. Couples are formed without fuss. We celebrate.

My major is from Odessa. He cannot believe I am Jewish. I still have my blue eyes, and my blonde hair has grown again. As I speak German and not Yiddish, he remains sceptical. He was recalled to the front before the unconditional surrender of the Great Reich.

During the night of 8–9 May, there is much knocking at our door. This time, it is victory, and the festivities start again and go on all night.

But it is also the end of an unforgettable encounter. Our men-friends receive their orders. For each one of us it remains only to decide where to go now. We can get back via Odessa or Berlin.

My major is too far away for me to make the first choice, and I don't want to go to Berlin. What is going to become of Germany, nobody knows at this stage. My parents had chosen France in the Nazi upheaval; they swore never again to set foot in a country which had betrayed them and driven them out. I will keep their oath. Germany no longer means anything to me. Hitler has exterminated all my people. I chose France once more and for ever.

13 · *The return*

Rosette and I chose to return by the quickest route; that is by joining up with the American army. To help us, our Soviet friends requisition two bicycles and two French prisoners-of-war.

I convince them that I know how to cycle. It is not true. At fourteen, during my last Easter vacation in Germany, I just about learned how to keep my balance and to cycle a bit. I have never since used a bicycle. The desire to do it was enough to make me manage but I came close to catastrophe.

The four of us are cycling smoothly along when a sharp descent suddenly appears. My speed increases and I am unable to use the brake. I take the lead, faster and faster, not knowing how to stop. Pierre dashes behind me, not knowing how to stop me, and it is he who falls into the pond, while I manage to brake with my feet and stop smoothly. Later on I will learn that to brake one only needs to pedal backwards.

The next obstacle is the bombed bridge across the Elbe. Neither Rosette nor I have the strength or acrobatic skill to cycle over it. She crosses first with Pierre and Franck, who carry their two bicycles. She then looks after them on the other bank while our two prisoners cross back to fetch me and the other bikes. I don't think I have ever crossed anywhere as dangerous as through the steel of this bridge which has collapsed in several places and through which we go up and down like tight-rope walkers.

With the help of the two men, we have no problem in requisitioning food and lodgings for ourselves in this no-man's land between two armies.

The first American soldier we come across confiscates the four bicycles, which we were counting on taking back to Paris. As I express myself better in English than in Yiddish, he is made to understand that we want to return to France as quickly as possible.

He finds us a goods train, in which the cattle-wagon we travel in differs only from the one on my convoy of 23 September 1942 in that it is not sealed with lead and there are only four of us in it, seated with the door open and our legs dangling outside. This train takes us to the town of Köten where the barracks are next to the airport. In front of the barracks two teams of American soldiers are playing a football match. Inside we are welcomed, as are all guests, with chocolate and cigarettes. At dinner we taste for the first time pasta 'à l'italienne', which is like a disgusting glue.

The next day we plead to be repatriated as soon as possible. The American campbeds are not at all comfortable and there aren't even enough to go round. Pierre and Franck had to sleep on the floor.

There are lots of people who want to get back to France. The only aeroplanes are small freight planes which bring supplies of kerosene and can take 25 people maximum on their return journey.

Lists of 25 names have to be prepared and typed. I set about this task, with everyone in agreement that the priority is the repatriation of deportees.

My list is soon ready and we take leave of our companions.

It is our first journey by air. The plane, which is small, flies low. We see the Rhine, then the Eiffel Tower. To please us, the pilot flies in a circle over Paris before landing at Le Bourget.

When we touch down, a band plays *La Marseillaise*. The national anthem rings out especially for us. While we listen, moved, men in white spray us with DDT, even going so far as to lift our skirts. Then we get into the same type of buses, inoffensive-looking and truly French, which took our people from the Vel d'Hiv to Drancy and from Drancy to the station where they left for the Final Solution.

I will never forget what the fascist government of Vichy was responsible for. The government of Pétain, Laval and so many others. Many have never been called to account for their crimes. There are guilty people running free, who still await the judgement of history. Indifference too was a criminal act.

The buses take us to the Hotel Lutétia. This is the place which has been chosen to welcome us and to give us back our identity. From here we will have to learn to live again – it will be difficult.

I am very different from how I was when I left. Deeply traumatised, I carry within me after-effects of my deportation which are as yet uncharted by medicine. At the same time, I come back richer in humanity and love of others. I know that one has to struggle to change the world, to struggle relentlessly. I have learned that human beings can become worse than beasts. Yet the Nazi concentration-camp system, unique in its kind, has failed. Humanity has triumphed over bestiality. Millions have died, having been tortured, assassinated, exterminated. Among those who were lucky to survive, men and women have surpassed themselves, thanks to the spirit of solidarity and resistance. Today most of them are dead. A handful still keep their memory alive and continue to demand that the human race should remain for ever on guard.

Epilogue

There was no one waiting for me. My whole family had been destroyed, the friends of my childhood and youth scattered. I had chosen France as my homeland for the second time but no address and no possessions remained.

The old flat at rue Nollet, emptied beforehand by the Gestapo, was now occupied by new tenants whom I had no desire to evict.

The idea of a rendezvous at the Coupole disappeared as each one was reabsorbed into their so-called normal life.

Rosette too had lost her father and mother but she still had some family. Her brother and sister-in-law welcomed us. We ate with them: our first meal of freedom, after leaving the Lutétia. I remember we had fish. When they wanted to throw away the leftovers, there were none: neither on Rosette's plate, nor on mine. Without a word, we ate the head, the tail and the bones along with the mouthwatering flesh.

We didn't know that we would never again be totally like other people. There is an invisible and intangible dividing line which puts survivors apart from the rest of humanity and creates between us indestructible bonds.

I was saved from despair by the immediate resumption of my studies under very difficult conditions. My one-time fellow students had completed their studies and were established, often in important posts.

At the laboratory of pathological anatomy, I received the same warm welcome, especially from Frédéric Busser, who helped me to choose a subject for my thesis.

My political involvement undoubtedly saved me twice: in the camps and on my return when it gave me a country.

The 34 months of sorrow, pain and terror have left deeper and more hidden scars than that made by my tattooed number. I was unable to have children. I had to wait until I was forty to build a home by adopting two children and creating a family in my country.

Life goes on, with strong hopes for the future, but 'our dead will only be avenged when there are no more killings'.*

*Inscription at the foot of the monument to Auschwitz, made by Françoise Salmon and located at the Père Lachaise cemetery, not far from the Wall of the Federation of Deportees.